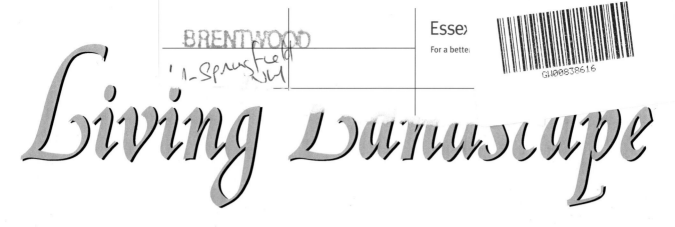

Living Landscape

Animals in Parks and Gardens of Essex

Essex Gardens Trust Research Group

Editor

Twigs Way

ESSEX GARDENS TRUST

Cover illustrations

Top Row (left to right)

Bee bole in garden wall, Eastbury Manor (photo: Tricia Moxey).

Dovecote and moat near Harlow (photo: Sally-Ann Turner).

New Peverels House (1611). (ERO D/DZT 5) (Reproduced by courtesy of the Essex Record Office.)

Middle Row (left to right)

British Library Add. MS 42130: Lutrell Psalter, f.176r, c.1325-35 (© The British Library Board. All Rights Reserved.)

Catherine Hyde, Duchess of Queensbury (after Charles Jervas). (Photo © English Heritage Photo Library.)

The Lady Rabbit Catchers (Royal MS 2 B VII: Queen Mary's Psalter f.155v, early C14 © The British Library Board. All Rights Reserved.)

Bottom Row (left to right)

Recommendations for the improvement of Wivenhoe Park (1765, detail). (ERO T/M 271) (Reproduced by courtesy of the Essex Record Office.)

Longhorn cow grazing in Epping Forest. (Courtesy of K. French)

Audley End and the Ring Hill Temple c.1788 by William Tomkins. (Photo © English Heritage Photo Library.)

Published by Essex Gardens Trust

ISBN 978-0-9565198-0-1

Copyright Essex Gardens Trust and Twigs Way 2010

www.gardenstrusts.org.uk/essex

Essex Gardens Trust is a registered charity, No 1057876

Design: John Williams

Contents

Dedication   2

Introduction   3
by Twigs Way

Abbreviations   4

Many a Luce in Stewe: Medieval Fishponds in Essex   5
by Michael Leach

Braxted Deer Park: From Larder to Landscape   12
by Fiona Wells

Seen but not Herd: Essex Deer Parks in the Calendar of
Patent Rolls (1232–1432), and Charter Rolls (1227–1516)   19
by Twigs Way

Fine Rich Conies or Pernicious Beasts : Rabbits in the Landscape   30
by Michael Leach

A Duffus in the Grounds: A Consideration of Some Essex Dovecotes   39
by Sally-Ann Turner

Honey Bees in Essex Gardens   50
by Tricia Moxey

'Tis Use Alone that Sanctifies Expense': Cattle, Beauty and Utility   59
by Ailsa Wildig

Historic Aviaries and Menageries: A Brief History and Some Essex Examples   68
by Jill Plater

The Essex Stable: Functional Building or Status Symbol?   74
by Penelope Keys

Animals in the Landscape: Thorndon Hall, Essex   82
by Robert Adams

Dedication

This publication is dedicated to Nancy Edwards (1929-2009) as a small recognition of her contributions to the work of the Essex Gardens Trust research group.

Nancy Edwards (née Briggs) was a distinguished historian who graduated at Oxford and was trained as an archivist at the Bodleian Library, before coming to work in the Essex Record Office in 1953. After early retirement in 1987, she actively supported the Essex Victoria County History, the local branch of the Historical Association, the Essex Society for Archaeology and History and the Essex Gardens Trust. After completing a biography of John Johnson, the eighteenth century Essex County surveyor and architect, she worked on a major study of the country houses of Essex which was nearly complete at her death. It is hoped that this will be published posthumously.

Nancy had a very sharp and enquiring mind and it is not surprising that her interest in country houses led to a keen interest in their surrounding gardens and parkland. Her active involvement with the research group was quite recent, but her contribution was immediate and incisive. She readily shared her extensive knowledge with tact and good humour and, not surprisingly, proved to be a resourceful and inspiring researcher in garden history. Her age was completely denied by her enthusiasm and her unflagging energy. Not long before her death, she was asked how she would like to be remembered, and she replied 'as one who tried to use her knowledge and skills to help others carry out historical research'. Every contributor to this publication benefited from this commitment and this dedication is a small recognition.

Introduction

Twigs Way

'A scene, however beautiful in itself, will soon lose its interest, unless it is enlivened by moving objects'
Humphry Repton (1806).[1]

Paintings, plans, descriptions and estate accounts, all record the important role once played by animals in designed landscapes. Buildings associated with animals litter our parks and gardens: stables, dairies, menageries, fishponds, deer shelters, beeboles and ha-has all give evidence of their once vibrant nature. But as livestock farming has declined in the agricultural landscape, so too has the inclusion of animals within the pleasure ground. The majestic stag or humble sheep which once provided colour and movement, have given way to silence and stillness, interrupted only by the stray muntjac or the inquisitive garden historian. Introducing motion into a designed landscape is a challenge which few land owners are willing to take up, and even fewer designers.

For Humphry Repton (1752-1818) the introduction of 'moving objects' into a garden or pleasure ground posed few problems. Cattle, deer, sheep, waterfowl, pheasants and even more exotic creatures, were usually readily available and acceptable to his clientele. Inclusion of animals within a park or pleasure ground had a well established tradition commencing with the deer parks, warrens and fishponds of the medieval period. During the eighteenth century the vogue for menageries, containing an assortment of animals from bears to zebu, was to culminate in the fashion for 'naturalisation' with the less dangerous animals allowed to roam free. Llamas, wallabies, and emus shared the grazing with surprised sheep. As day-to-day travel and traction was also provided by horses and oxen the 'scene' on many estates was not so much enlivened by moving objects as positively heaving.

Garden historians and archaeologists have long recognised animals as an element of the historic landscape, undertaking research into documentary records and physical remains. Since the 1980s considerable work has been carried out, usually at county level, on deer parks, dovecotes and fishponds as vital elements of the 'elite landscape'. As a result of this research there has been much greater appreciation of the role animals played in social and political landscaping, whether through creation of a deer park or conspicuous display of 'improved' cattle. In Essex, work by John Hunter has laid a foundation which subsequent studies on deer parks have benefited from, including those by Wells and Way in this volume. However, other elements have had less attention paid to them in the past. In the present volume, Tricia Moxey's study of bee keeping in Essex is the first to be carried out by a garden historian in the county, whilst Sally-Ann Turner's work on dovecotes not only updates recording carried out in the 1930s, but asks the question 'how do historic dovecotes 'fit' in modern garden designs? Other elements of the 'elite landscape' package are also represented in articles on warrens and fishponds by Michael Leach, crossing over between landscape archaeology and garden history.

As garden history has matured and developed, so has the areas of enquiry which it addresses and the techniques it uses. Geographic Information Systems (GIS) and associated fieldwork techniques allow faster and more detailed recording as demonstrated in the present study of animal-related structures at Thorndon Hall. Understanding and implementing new techniques and approaches can be difficult for small volunteer groups who may not have access to technological innovations, and the Essex Gardens Trust are very fortunate to have close links with Writtle College and the expertise of Robert Adams. Penelope Keys, also a Writtle student, has used traditional methods to analyse the development of stables in Essex elite landscapes, but her thoughtful approach has resulted in much new material on spatial location and design of stables in relation to the country house. This fresh approach is also seen in the article by Ailsa Wildig, where paintings and texts have been brought together to examine the role of cattle in landscape design.

When this volume was first planned, the work on menageries and aviaries was to be carried out respectively by Nancy Edwards and Jill Plater, both key members of the EGT research team. It was a huge shock to us all to hear of Nancy's untimely death, and the immediate response was to try and complete the work which she had commenced. Jill Plater has valiantly combined the two subjects in her study.

The research presented in this volume was inspired by the Essex Gardens Trust year of Animals in the Landscape. To paraphrase Humphry Repton, our object is that it will hold your interest and enliven your understanding of the Essex landscape.

Twigs Way
(January 2010)

---

1 Repton, H 1806, *An Enquiry into the Changes of Taste in Landscape Gardening: to which are added some observations on its theory and practice including a defence of the art* (Taylor: London), 101-102

Abbreviations

BL	British Library
CCR	Calendar of Close Rolls, HMSO
CLR	Calendar of Liberate Rolls, HMSO
CPR	Calendar of Patent Rolls, HMSO
EAH	*Essex Archaeology & History*
EAT, ns	*Transactions of the Essex Archaeological Society,* new series
EC	*Essex Countryside*
ERO	Essex Record Office
Essex HER	Essex Historic Environment Record
JAC	*Journal of Architectural Conservation*
RCHM	Royal Commission on Historical Monuments (Essex)
TAMS	*Transactions of the Ancient Monuments Society*
VA	*Vernacular Architecture*

Many a Luce in Stewe:
Medieval Fishponds in Essex

Michael Leach
2 Landview Gardens, Ongar, Essex CM5 9EQ

Ful many a fat partrich hadde he in muwe
And many a breeme and many a luce in stewe[1]
(prologue to Chaucer's *Canterbury Tales*)

Introduction

Freshwater fish were a high status food in the medieval period, and their means of production were the preserve of the wealthy. Although innumerable pieces of water - including medieval moats - have been loosely identified as fishponds, it was essential for successful fish breeding that ponds should possess a number of specific features which are discussed in this article. Lack of maintenance means that many medieval fishponds are now dry and are only visible as minor earthworks, but many can still be positively identified from these distinctive features. A selection of medieval fishponds attached to royal manors and monastic establishments in Essex are critically examined, and their significance in the designed landscape – as well as their post-medieval adaptation or loss – is discussed. Other evidence of fishpond management that has been found in the primary and secondary sources that were examined during this study is included.

Early History of Fishponds in England

In medieval England, freshwater fish were the food of the wealthy. Chaucer's Franklin, an unashamed parvenue, was demonstrating his new social status with 'many a breeme and many a luce in stewe' [luce = pike, stew = fishpond]. Hunting and fishing were pastimes of the rich who were likely to be envied, or attacked, by critics of privilege. Fish were high status presents and the ponds for breeding and storing them were formidably expensive to construct and maintain. Rearing fish for the table was a slow process – at least five years for bream to reach a suitable size, for example. Carp could be raised to edible size in three years, but these fish were not introduced until the fifteenth century. For these reasons, security was of great importance and medieval fishponds were usually overlooked by a building to provide protection from human predators.[2] The oft-cited religious obligation to abstain from meat on Fridays and Saturdays, the 40 days of Lent and various other festivals (amounting to nearly half the days of the year in the fourteenth century) would have had little impact on the peasantry who mainly subsisted on cereals.[3] Though the wealthy certainly consumed considerable amounts of fish, much came from the sea, often preserved by being salted, smoked or air-dried. The 1431/2 accounts of John de Vere, earl of

Oxford (whose household spent much of its time in Essex) reveal a consumption of only 215 freshwater fish, in contrast to more than 26,000 salt-water fish.[4] A century later the inventory of Sir William Petre's saltfish store at Ingatestone Hall, Essex, listed over 175 'couple' of various salt or dried sea fish. These had been bought in Essex markets, as well as at Stourbridge Fair in Cambridgeshire.[5] Fresh water fish were often kept for particular occasions, and were reserved for the guests at the high table. When Edward IV visited the duchess of Buckingham at Writtle, Essex, in 1465, their meal included eight pike and six tench.[6]

It would be a mistake to presume that all fresh water fish came from fishponds – many were trapped or netted in local rivers and kept alive until needed in the domestic fishpond or stew. Domesday Book lists some 25 fish weirs in Essex, as well as a number of other inland fishing sites.[7] Sir William Petre's accounts in 1555 show payments made to men for fishing the rivers at Ingatestone and in Waltham Forest; the latter expedition on a single day yielded four pike, a 'great carp' and a dish of roach.[8] Nevertheless, fishponds were an important part of the medieval and early modern landscape. As freshwater fish was a high status food, its means of production were worthy of display in the vicinity of the mansion, as a visible and conspicuous demonstration the owner's power and wealth. Water was highly valued for its ornamental qualities in medieval landscape designs. Some high status sites, such as Woodham Walter Hall and Clavering Castle, both in Essex, were surrounded by a complex series of ponds, lakes and leats of far greater complexity than was necessary for maintaining fishponds. Such ornamental waters would have also contained fish as they were decorative objects in the garden setting (raised terraces and mounds might be provided for viewing them) as well as being handy for the kitchens! The less wealthy built moats, though not all moated sites surrounded a house. Some had a purely ornamental function and were used for the conspicuous display of the orchards, rabbit warrens, gardens and pigeon houses of their owners. The function of any piece of water changed and developed over time - the medieval fishpond was often modified to provide an ornamental lake in an eighteenth century landscaped park, or to cater for the sport of coarse fishing which grew from the sixteenth century onwards. Bourne Mill, Colchester, which had been a source of fish for the monastic refectory, was later adapted by its lay owners. The medieval mill was replaced by an elaborate fishing lodge. Fishponds, therefore, should not be seen simply as a means of keeping and rearing fish, but looked at in the broader context of the developing history of designed landscape.

Design and Construction of Fishponds

Though fish can survive in reasonably aerated water, their efficient rearing depends on four specific requirements. These dictated the construction of ponds which were intended primarily for fish, and can provide useful criteria for identifying medieval fishponds.[9]

The first requirement was to have an incoming supply of water from river or stream, both to provide aeration and to supply a source of micro-organisms to feed the fish. This might require the diversion of streams, or the construction of leats. Many ponds which have been labelled as fishponds lack a supply of running water, making it unlikely that they could have been used as such. It is often assumed that moats were used for keeping fish but many lacked this essential, and would not have been satisfactory for the purpose. Numerically Essex has more moated sites of medieval origin than any other county and their purpose continues to be a matter of debate.[10] A few moats, however, did have a supply of running water from a river or stream, and were provided with an attached pond which could have acted as a stew (a store for keeping fish, and for reducing their muddy flavour prior to consumption), or as a place for breeding or fattening. It is apparent that some moats were very productive. A theft from the moat of Horham Hall at Thaxted, Essex, in 1693 removed '60 carps and other fish worth £6'.[11] Another Essex example is the abandoned manorial site at Slades, Navestock, where there is evidence of two heavily silted rectangular fishponds with traces of sluices, adjoining the homestead moat which was fed by the valley stream. The symmetry of these ponds, and their position adjacent to the moat, show that they were intended to have a visual impact in addition to their practical use.[12]

The second requirement was an effective overflow or sluice to control the level of each pond. Flood water poses a serious threat to dams and it was essential to prevent damage from water flowing over the top. Overflows had to be protected from erosion and blockages and it is certain that poorly maintained systems often resulted in dam failure. The dams themselves were constructed by ramming earth between two or three lines of partly charred oak or elm piles, with brushwood woven between them. The charring was probably intended to protect the timber from rot, though permanently water-logged timber (particularly elm) has a surprisingly long life. A sixteenth century fish manual recommended the subsequent planting of osiers or willows to strengthen dams and pond edges.[13]

The third requirement was the ability to manage each pool independently of its neighbours. This enabled an individual pool to be drained, both to harvest and sort the fish into different sizes, as well as for periodic removal of silt. Many of the fish manuals advocated leaving an emptied pond dry for up to twelve months, every three or four years, and even taking a crop of oats off the exposed bottom. Recently cleaned ponds were considered to be the most productive.[14] The 1591 Walker map of Moulsham Hall, Chelmsford, shows three fishponds in the park – two are coloured blue, one brown. It has been suggested that the latter had been drained and was lying fallow at the time the survey was made.[15] Documentary references to this practice are rare, but the Essex diarist, Ralph Josselin, noted on 2 August 1651 that he 'cast the water out of the pond on the greene, and cast out the mudde'.[16] Occasionally the ability to drain ponds worked against the interests of the owner; in 1610 fish thieves cut the head of a millpond at Terling and made off with an unspecified quantity of fish.[17] Another spectacular theft in 1641 involved pulling up the sluice of Lord Petre's pond at Thorndon Park and 'making off with at least 500 carps and other fish worth at least £20'. One has to wonder if these were professional thieves as, at the same time, they took another £10 worth of fish from a pond on nearby Childerditch Common.[18] The transportation and disposal of this quantity of fish must have required considerable organisation.

The fourth requirement was for a variety of ponds (or at least a range of shallow areas within a main pond) in order to provide different habitats, and to protect young fish or spawn from predators. Different adult species had different requirements – carp, for example, liked a gravel or sandy bottom, whereas tench and eels favoured mud. Carp and tench were said to thrive best in the absence of rival species. Bream were very fertile, and pike were often combined with them in order to thin out the young, and to allow the survivors to fatten more effectively. Other species, however, could be severely depleted by this predator. It was recommended that ponds for fattening should be about five feet deep, with steep sides to discourage attempts to breed, and a deeper central trench to provide a refuge for large fish, as well as to deter human fish thieves. Ponds needed to be drained to sort the fish into different sizes for distribution to other ponds, and in order to reduce losses from predation by larger fish. By the eighteenth century, narrow ponds were recommended so that, after drainage, the accumulated silt could be thrown out by a labourer onto the bank in a single toss. Fish were fattened on curds, grains, animal blood, and the fresh entrails of rabbits or chickens.[19] Stew ponds, already referred to, were convenient for short term storage before eating, and also to remove the muddy taste from river fish. These diverse requirements help to explain the archaeological complexity of some medieval fishponds, whose construction and management would have required considerable skill and a large outlay of capital.

Leats and ponds are common requirements for fish farming and for water mills, and it would seem obvious to include both in one enterprise. Millers often fished their own millponds for profit, and sometimes their rents were partly paid in eels. However there were conflicting requirements, as ponds for the cultivation of fish had to be emptied and left fallow periodically, whereas the miller required a reliable and constant supply of water. It is not clear how these conflicting interests were reconciled. There may have been a slack periods for milling, particularly in the summer months before the new harvest came in, and this could have been an opportune time to empty the pond for cleaning and sorting out the stock. However, leaving a pond fallow for 6 to 12 months would have been incompatible with the needs of the miller. An Essex example of combined mill and fishponds is at Bourne Mill in Colchester, an outlying property belonging to St John's abbey, and this is discussed below.

Many pond designs are now very hard to interpret. Some have been damaged or erased by repairs, or significantly altered by later modifications or improvements (as at Audley End). Others have been partly obliterated by silting up, dam rupture and return to agricultural use (as at Clavering Castle, and Radwinter Hall). Occasionally the substantial earthworks prevented subsequent cultivation and the site has been preserved under dense vegetation (as at Woodham Walter Hall). Usually their details can only be revealed by careful survey or aerial photography and many abandoned fishponds will only be only evident to the observant eye as faint banks or crop marks. However their form, and their proximity to a source of water and a dwelling, should suggest their original purpose. Due to the very large number of possible sites, this study will be confined to a few examples of medieval fishponds from royal and monastic sites – but it is hoped that the principles of fishpond construction and management that have been discussed will lead to a better understanding of other potential sites in Essex.

Royal fishponds

There were three royal manors with fishponds in Essex, of which the most important was that at Havering Palace which had belonged to the crown since before the Conquest. It was used by various monarchs and their consorts from the twelfth century, and Charles I was the last sovereign to reside here in 1638. A survey of 1650 found that the buildings were dilapidated and thoroughly old-fashioned. Though some repairs were done by a tenant after the Restoration, by the early 1700s the palace was uninhabitable. A century later, nothing remained visible above ground.[20] Little is known about the gardens which were on the west side, though a survey of 1596 gives a tantalising glimpse of what must have been a walled and locked pleasance:

'In the Gardein: three double locks, the alleys and quarters laid out and sett w^t quicksett and sweet briar, w^t cherye trees, aple trees, and others out of repayre'.[21]

Though occupation by royalty may have been intermittent, the park was used during the Middle Ages for hunting and for providing meat, wood, timber and fish for the royal household and their beneficiaries. Two wild boars were introduced in 1223 and their descendants were still in the park four decades later.[22] In the mid thirteenth century the royal table was taking an average of 44 fallow deer annually from the park.[23] In 1221 the abbess of Barking was given leave to hunt foxes in Havering Park.[24]

Provision of fish (particularly bream), both for the royal household and for favoured subjects, was an important function of the estate in the thirteenth century, and substantial numbers were provided. In 1251, for example, payments were made for removing 400 bream from the Havering pond, and for their carriage to the royal palaces at Windsor and Kempton.[25] It was not unusual to send live fish by road to stock a fishpond elsewhere. These were transported in water in barrels lined with canvas.[26] In 1232 it was noted that the Havering fishpond was in such poor condition that all the fish had died, and instructions were sent for the pond to be drained and cleaned.[27] Other repairs were ordered in 1246, 1254 and 1264.[28] There must have been a substantial pond or ponds to accommodate the 3000 pike ordered from the sheriff of Cambridgeshire in 1250.[29] There was also a stew near the palace kitchens for the short-term storage of fish destined for the table.[30]

As the palace was on high ground, and ponds for breeding and fattening would have required a supply of running water, the fishponds must have been situated on or near the river Rom, a mile to the west. A plan of the Liberty of Havering of c.1618 shows two possible sites on the Rom within Havering Park – 'the greate poole' near Great Lodge and a moated site at Little Lodge. There is also 'the newe pond' on a tributary of the Rom,[31] but this is remote from any buildings, making it unlikely that it was a fishpond. The park was split in the seventeenth century and returned to farmland, and a new model dairy farm was built on or near the site of Little Lodge in the mid nineteenth century.[32] Neither the 'greate poole' nor the moated site can be found on modern maps, but reference to the 1618 plan suggests that they may have been at or near what is now Foreberry Wood South and Foreberry Wood North respectively. The North Wood contains no recognisable embankments or excavations and, as it slopes gently upwards to the west, would have been an unlikely site for a pond. In contrast, South Wood is in a valley bottom and its southern end contains a confusion of substantial earthworks. Some are steep and poorly vegetated embankments of recent construction but, hidden behind them is a fragment of a much older bank of a more gentle profile which might have been part of the dam of the 'greate poole'. The Rom runs below it in a straight line (with no sign of a corresponding embankment on the other side of the stream), and it may have been cut to drain the area after the destruction of the main dam. A wet area some distance to the north of the old dam bank may mark the course of the fishpond leat.

The second Essex royal manor was at Writtle. King John built the so-called King John's Hunting Lodge at Writtle in 1211.[33] This was a moated site, fed by a stream, with a group of three separate fishponds to the east. Repairs were ordered in 1270 to the 'king's stew at Writtle'.[34] Both moat and ponds have survived (in somewhat modified form) within the grounds of Writtle College. There is no medieval documentary evidence of fish being taken from the Writtle ponds but the royal lodge was tenanted for much of the medieval period until it was granted to Sir William Petre in 1554. By then, or shortly afterwards, the buildings had been levelled and the area returned to agricultural use. In recent times the site has been landscaped to form part of the college grounds. An imaginative reconstruction of the site in 1305 was published in 1993 in *Essex Archaeology & History*.[35]

The third royal manor was at Newport in the north of the county. The fishpond here is mainly known through the record of extensive repairs that were being undertaken early in the thirteenth century, requiring some 50 oak trees. In 1240 the 'good men of Newport' were instructed to carry out further repairs to the 'pond and bays of the king's fish stew'.[36] The reference to 'bays' suggests that sheltered areas had been constructed for rearing small fish or fry. In December 1240 and 1241, the men of Newport were instructed to receive all the fish caught by William, the royal fisherman, and to transport them to the royal household at Westminster for the Christmas festivities.[37] The manor, though granted to numerous different tenants at different times, remained in royal hands until 1550. Towards the end of that century Norden noted 'Newporte, called Newporte Ponde, of a ponde at yᵉ ende of yᵉ towne, now firm ground'.[38]

By this period, the manorial tenants had become accustomed to grazing their cattle here, a practice regulated by the manorial court. Problems arose on several occasions when lords of the manor attempted to enclose parts of the land, and their newly erected fences were pulled down, and the ditches backfilled. Eventually a compromise was reached – the lord was allowed the first crop of hay in exchange for a cash payment, and the tenants were allowed to graze a limited number of beasts from August to February.[39]

Morant noted that Norden's dry pond was sited at the south end of the town.[40] It is generally agreed that this was the abandoned royal fishpond, the site of which has been identified as the town's present recreation field, situated south of Station Road and east of the High Street. The water would probably have been visible to travellers passing along the main road between London and Cambridge. On the east side of the site is the River Cam, which now runs in a deeply cut man-made channel. This cut may be relatively modern (and perhaps built for flood prevention) as the red brick bridge carrying Station Road across it has a date stone of 1858, and bears the names of the churchwardens. There are various irregularities in the recreation field, including a shallow east-west bank about 100m to the south of Station Road, but it is not clear if these are related to fishpond management, or to later enclosures made after the pond was drained. There is no sign of the leat that would have been required to feed the pond, but the south end of the field is now very overgrown.

None of the three royal Essex fishponds seem to have supplied fish to the court after the thirteenth century, though doubtless the tenants would have continued to use them to supply their own kitchens. It seems that it had become simpler to obtain fish from commercial sources, rather than bringing it in from distant royal manors.

Monastic fishponds

Monastic requirement for fish would suggest that all sites would have had a fishpond, though it must be remembered that a great deal of salted and dried sea fish was eaten. It is possible that religious houses near the coast would have relied entirely on sea or estuary fish. Beeleigh abbey, for example, which is on the tidal part of the River Blackwater, has only a single small pond shown on early maps, fed by a spring arising higher up the hillside. The ponds within the present day garden are all of twentieth century origin.[41] Presumably the Blackwater would have provided an easy and regular supply of fresh fish and the single pond may have been a stew for short term storage. Some of the inland houses, such as Waltham abbey and Tilty abbey, were well provided with flowing water both for domestic and sanitary purposes, as well as for fishponds and a monastic mill.[42] Other sites, such as Latton priory and Thoby priory, were without an obvious source of running water, but must have been dependant on springs for their water supply, and they too appear to have had fishponds.[43] After the dissolution, the new lay owners of sites such as Prittlewell priory, Southend and St John's abbey, Colchester, adapted monastic ponds as part of their landscaped grounds.

At Prittlewell priory, parts of the conventual buildings survived within a private house whose gardens and park were laid out within the precinct. There are now two large rectangular ponds of roughly equal size and shape in the priory grounds, believed to be remains of monastic fishponds. They lie side by side, and are placed end-on to a stream at a lower level which would have been used as an overflow, or for periodical drainage. The ponds are fed by a spring, and are now connected together at the lower end by a breach in the dividing bank. Evidence from maps indicates that these ponds have been modified in a relatively recent times. A map of 1777 shows two separate ponds in the same position as the present ones, but both are irregular in shape, that to the south being the larger.[44] In 1869 the ponds were of similar irregular shape. They would have had ornamental value at this time, as one of the access drives to the house passed between the two, though the ponds themselves were not specifically described in the sales particulars.[45] When sold 20 years later, the arrangement was unaltered, but the more detailed particulars mentioned a thatched boathouse, and a similarly roofed ice house, which is shown on the sales plan between the upper ends of the two ornamental lakes.[46] After the First World War, the site was acquired by Southend Corporation. The mansion opened as a museum in 1922 and the park was laid out for public use. It was probably at this time that the ponds were re-cut to their present regular shape, and connected together at the lower end. The drive was abolished and there is now no trace of the bridge that would have carried it across the stream.

The foundation charter of St John's abbey, Colchester, dated 1096, records the donation of two fishponds and a mill which Morant identified as Bourne Mill.[47] The mill is now owned by the National Trust and lies south of the town on a stream arising from a spring a short distance to the west. Though the stream is now very modest, there were, by the eighteenth century, two further mills a short distance downstream, so its flow may have been more substantial in the past. Evidence from nineteenth century maps shows that there were two ponds, one above the other, and this may have been a necessary arrangement, in this narrow valley, to store sufficient water to drive the mill. The upper pond (whose site is now covered by woodland) had a bypass channel, so it could have been filled and drained independently as a fishpond. There is no evidence of such a channel for the lower pond, though drainage through the mill sluice would have been possible, perhaps (in order to reduce inconvenience to the miller) at a time when the mill was not busy. Medieval leases of this mill did not stipulate rent in fish, but the management of the fishing may have been in the hands of the monks or another lessee. By the eighteenth century, the mill leases excluded the fishing rights which were retained by the owner, almost certainly for sport rather than fish farming. The mill remained in royal hands for a few years after the abbey's dissolution in 1538, and then passed through various owners until its acquisition by Sir Thomas Lucas in 1590. His father had acquired the main site of St John's abbey in nearby Colchester as the family residence and it has been suggested that the purchase of Bourne Mill was a status-driven move to re-unite the former monastic estate. Sir Thomas promptly rebuilt the mill as an exuberantly ornate lodge with oversized Flemish gables, obelisk pinnacles and an octagonal chimney shaft. This was an ostentatious designed landscape feature, which would have been used by the Lucas family as a fishing lodge or banqueting house. It was provided with two fireplaces with four-centred arches, and had a fine view over the water. Mill machinery was installed on the lower floor, though by the early seventeenth century it was being used for fulling, which required less space than corn milling.[48]

Ponds associated with former monastic houses may not be of medieval origin and those to the north of Leez priory are an example. Here the River Ter runs in a re-entrant curve for 2km and is lined with a chain of 12 ponds, entirely in the parish of Felsted. A site visit in June 2009 showed that all but one of the ponds is now dry. Though most of the dams survive as incomplete banks across the east side of the valley floor, the western part has been destroyed by cultivation. Three of the dams survive intact, two carrying minor roads and one forming a farm track. They are about 2m high at the centre, and about 9m across the base. In order to construct this line of ponds on the valley floor, the stream itself was diverted into a deep leat above the ponds on the east side of the valley, and retained in this position by a substantial bank. The top of the retaining bank is about 5m wide and, in several places, it appears to have been terraced. The leat, through which the River Ter still flows, is nearly 2.5 km in length and is, in places, over 2m above the level of the valley floor. On the opposite side of the valley from the leat, there is an angling lake of twentieth century construction.

The usual assumption, from Morant onwards, has been that these were fishponds belonging to the priory,

though the 1921 RCHM volume described them as millponds.[49] Their size is without precedent for the latter function, and on a far larger scale than would be necessary for driving a mill.[50] They were also far too big for the rearing and cultivation of fish. Though there are examples of chains of monastic fishponds elsewhere (such as Halesowen, Worcestershire and Owston, Leicestershire), none are on anything like this scale.[51] The Leez ponds also fail to meet one of the principal requirements of a medieval fishpond. Being sited across the valley floor, it would not have been possible to provide a bypass channel to allow the ponds to be drained and managed independently of each other.

Though it is clear that they were dry by Morant's time, their date of construction is uncertain. The area they occupy is shown as a paled park on Norden's Essex map of 1594, and there is a documentary reference in 1595 to a 'Ponde Park' at Leez Priory.[52] In 1909 French concluded that, as the priory appeared to be in the dry bed of a thirteenth lake, the ponds must have pre-dated the foundation of the priory in the early thirteenth century and, on rather tenuous evidence, concluded that they were prehistoric.[53] Another contemporary historian believed that what French had taken to be pond banks had been constructed as flood protection, to defend the low-lying monastic site from the nearby River Ter.[54] The evidence suggests that the primary function of this chain of lakes was not for fish production or milling, but that it was a high status landscape feature. In 1381 the priory was licensed to 'enclose 100 acres of land and wood in Little Leghes, without the metes of the forest, make a park thereof, and hold the same in perpetuity'.[55] Though this park cannot now be identified with any certainty, it was in a different parish. Leez was not a rich priory[56] and it seems unlikely that it would have needed - or been able to afford - another park It is much more likely that Pond Park dates from the time of the ruthlessly acquisitive Sir Richard Rich who was granted the priory and its surrounding land in 1536. He demolished many of the monastic buildings and erected a new brick mansion round two courtyards as his principal country residence. He would surely have wanted an appropriate setting for his impressive new mansion. More than a century later, in 1673, the estate was described in the funeral sermon of one of Rich's descendants as 'a secular Elysium, a worldly paradise, a heaven upon earth if there be any such'.[57] Even allowing for the normal funeral hyperbole, there must have been a spectacular parkland setting of which now almost no evidence remains.

By c.1720 the estate had been partially disparked, a process completed after 1753 when it was sold to Guy's Hospital.[58] Much of Rich's mansion was demolished and the parkland, with its ponds, were returned to agricultural use. An estate map of Pond Park Farm of c.1775 shows that the ponds had gone, the only trace being the name of Pond Head Field.[59] The surrounding field boundaries are irregular and well supplied with standard trees and John Hunter concluded that they represented much earlier enclosure boundaries, which had been retained by Rich to provide game cover, and re-used subsequently as field boundaries when the estate was disparked.[60] Early in the nineteenth century the condition of these ponds was described by Arthur Young

'I have not often seen instances of such neglect of ponds ... as is the case of Leighs-Priory... There is a chain of them, nearly a mile in length, and occupying about 30 acres, which were once under water; formed and sluiced with great attention, and a stream through them; but at present, and for many years past, water only in two of them, and those almost choked up with mud by neglect. This of all the other branches of rural economy, is the least practised and least understood in England; yet fish is everywhere a great luxury, and sells at a high price.'[61]

So the most impressive ponds in Essex are almost certainly not monastic, with their primary function as a spectacular contribution to the park landscape. Their size would have made them unsuitable for fish cultivation but might have provided for the growing popularity of the sport of angling which, unlike today, seems to have been enjoyed by people of quality of both sexes. Few would now regard angling as part of the courtship ritual, but Edmund Waller (1606-1687) noted its flirtatious possibilities in 'Poem on St James's Park, lately improved by his Majesty'.

'Beneath, a shole of silver fishes glides,
And plays about the gilded barge's side;
The ladies, angling in the chrystal lake,
Feast on the waters with their prey they take:
At once victorious with their lines and eyes,
They make the fishes and the men their prize'.[62]

Conclusion

This essay has outlined the practical requirements that were needed for managed medieval fishponds, as well as the importance of such ponds in the medieval designed landscape, with some examples from Essex royal manors and monastic foundations.

Familiarity with the practical features necessary for the efficient management of fishponds may help to identify many more former sites, as well as excluding others which may have been incorrectly designated. Those medieval ponds that have survived have undergone subsequent modification to adapt them as parkland features, or for the sport of fishing which developed from the sixteenth century onwards. However, as Arthur Young noted, raising fish for food was a largely forgotten skill by the end of the eighteenth century. Ponds which failed to find an alternative use under their new gentry owners would have been eventually lost from the accumulation of silt or breached dams, and the land returned to agricultural use. Such ponds are now more likely to be noticed by the field archaeologist than the garden historian.

Undoubtedly much remains to be discovered and elucidated about particular sites and the use of fishponds in the designed medieval landscape.

Bibliography (including Primary Sources)

Aberg, F.A., 1978 *Medieval Moated Sites,* CBA Research Report, 17

Andrews, D. & Gilman, P., 1992 'Tilty Abbey: a note on the surviving remains' in *EAH,* 23

Anon, 1767 *The Complete Grazier, or Gentleman and Farmer's Directory,* London

Anon, 1770 *History of Essex from a Late Survey by a Gentleman,* Chelmsford

Benson, L.D. (ed), 1987 *The Riverside Chaucer,* OUP

Bettley, J., & Pevsner, N., 2007 *The Buildings of England: Essex,* Yale UP

Bond, C.J., 1988 'Monastic Fisheries' in Aston M. (ed) *Medieval Fish, Fisheries and Fishponds in England,* BAR British Series

Chapman & Andre, 1777 map of Essex

Christy, M., 1907 'The Freshwater fisheries of Essex' in *ER,* 15

Clapham, A.W., 1914 'The Augustinian Priory of Little Leez' in *EAT,* ns, 13

Cooper J. (ed), 1994 *Victoria County History of Essex,* 9, OUP

Dyer, C., 1988 'Consumption of Fish in Medieval England' in Aston, M. (ed), *Medieval Fish, Fisheries and Fishponds in England,* BAR British Series

Emmison F.G., 1970 *Tudor Secretary: Sir William Petre at Court and Home,* Phillimore

Fowler, R.C., 1904 'Inventories of Essex Monasteries in 1536' in *EAT,* ns, 9

French, J., 1909 'On the High Antiquity of the Lakes at Leighs Priory' in *EAT,* ns, 11

Huggins, P., 1972 'Excavations at Waltham Abbey 1970-72' in *EAH,* 4

Hunter, J.M., 1993 'King John's hunting-lodge at Writtle' in *EAH,* 24

Hunter, J.M., 1994a 'Medieval & Tudor Parks of Middle Chelmer Valley' in *EAH ,* 25

Hunter, J.M., 1994b 'Littley Park, Great Waltham – historical survey' in *EAH,* 25

Leach, M., 2009 unpublished report of site visit to Beeleigh Abbey

Macfarlane, A., 1991 *The Diary of Ralph Josselin 1616-1683,* British Academy

Morant P., 1758 *History and Antiquities of Colchester,* London

Morant, P., 1768 *History of Essex,* London

Norden, J., 1594 *Speculae Britanniae Pars* (ed. Ellis, Sir H., Camden Society, 1840)

Nurse, B., et al., 1995 *A Village in Time – the history of Newport,* Newport News

Ogborne, E., 1814 *The History of Essex,* London

Powell, W.R. (ed) 1978 *Victoria County History of Essex,* 7, OUP

Rackham, O., 1993 *The History of the Countryside*, Dent

Roberts, B.K., 1988 'The Re-Discovery of Fish Ponds' in Aston, M. (ed), *Medieval Fish, Fisheries & Fish Ponds*, BAR British Series

Steane, J.M., 1988 'Royal Fishponds of Medieval England' in Aston M (ed), *Medieval Fish, Fisheries and Fishponds in England*, BAR British Series

Suckling, A., 1845 *Memorials of the Antiquities & Architecture of Essex*, London

Thornton, C.C., 2007 unpublished report on Bourne Mill for the National Trust

Walton, I. & Cotton, C., 1815 *The Complete Angler*, London (with fishpond advice based on Lebault's *Maison Rustique* published in Lyons in 1594)

Young, A., 1807 *General View of the Agriculture of Essex*, London

References

1 Benson 1987, 29
2 Rackham 1993, 366
3 Dyer 1988, 27
4 Dyer 1988, 30
5 Emmison 1970, 139
6 Dyer 1988, 34
7 Christy 1907, 70
8 Emmison 1970, 224
9 Roberts 1988, 9-26
10 Aberg 1978, 3
11 ERO: Q/SR 479/59
12 RCHM 1921, ii, 192
13 Walton 1815, 345
14 Bond 1988, 99
15 ERO: D/DM P2
16 Macfarlane 1991, 253
17 ERO: Q/SR 191/17
18 ERO: D/DP/L36/26
19 Anon 1767, 244-51; Walton 1815, 345
20 Powell 1978, 14
21 Ogborne 1814, 115
22 Rackham 1993, 37
23 ibid, 126
24 ibid, 125
25 CLR 1245-51, 341
26 CLR 1240-45, 281
27 CCR 1232, 76
28 CLR 1245-51, 42; ibid 1251-56, 177; ibid 1267-72, 120
29 CLR 1245-51, 293
30 Bond 1988, 56
31 Powell 1978, 11-13
32 VCH 1978, vii, 11-13
33 Morant 1768, ii, 61
34 CLR 1267-72, 120
35 Hunter 1993, 122
36 CLR 1240-45, 2
37 Steane 1988, 61; CLR 1240-45, 15 & 97
38 Norden 1594, 22
39 Nurse 1995, 38-9
40 Morant 1768, ii, 584
41 Leach, 2009
42 Huggins, 1972, 36; Andrews & Gilman, 1992, 157.
43 Essex HER no. 23; Suckling 1845, 44
44 Chapman & Andre, 1777, sheet XXIII
45 ERO D/DNe T42/12 & D/DS 84/2
46 ERO D/DS 25
47 Morant 1758, ii, 33
48 Thornton 2007, 6-28; Bettley & Pevsner 2007, 299; Cooper 1994, 260
49 Morant 1768, ii, 100; RCHM ii, 84
50 John Bedington (professional miller), personal communication
51 Bond 1988, 100
52 Norden 1594; ERO D/DB 11/12/1
53 French 1909, 162-3
54 Clapham 1914, 211, 215
55 CPR 4 Richard II, 608
56 Fowler, 1904. 281
57 Anon 1770, 348
58 Hunter 1994b, 119-20
59 ERO D/DZ 19
60 Hunter 1994a, 116
61 Young 1807, ii, 369
62 Walton 1815, 345

Braxted Deer Park: From Larder to Landscape

Fiona Wells

Homestead Farm, Radwinter, Saffron Walden, Essex CB10 2UA

Introduction

Essex was one of the most densely imparked counties in medieval England, its proximity to London making it an attractive location in which to hold land. Incorporating new research and earlier unpublished lists, John Hunter and Oliver Rackham recorded the creation/presence of 156 deer parks in the county between 1086 and 1600.[1] It is probable that there are further parks yet to be discovered in the county via a close examination of the actual text of calendared Patent, Charter and Close Rolls combined with local archive work (see also Way in this volume).

Few medieval parks were to be found in the Dengie Hundred but otherwise, they were fairly evenly distributed across the county with perhaps a slightly higher density along the interface of the London clay and the chalky boulder clays of the lower Chelmer valley. Parks varied enormously in size. Examples ranging from the licence granted c.1248 to Philip Basset to impark ten acres close to the boundary of the Great Park at Ongar, to the Royal Park of one thousand three hundred acres in Havering-atte-Bower. No two parks were the same, but deer were a feature of the majority of medieval parks – their presence and the hunting opportunity that they provided re-enforcing the social status of the owner.

In this paper I shall consider the transition from medieval deer park to post medieval designed landscape at Braxted Park near Witham, Essex. Examination of the archives for the site has provided a tantalizing (although not detailed) insight into the changing role of deer in the landscape between the thirteenth and eighteenth centuries. Braxted Park provides an interesting case study as it is one of less than ten parks in Essex that successfully made the transition from medieval deer park to later landscape park.

Background

Medieval parks are perhaps most commonly thought of as enclosures for the keeping of deer, initially the native red and roe deer. From the late eleventh century, Anglo-Norman aristocrats re-introduced the fallow deer to this country following the example set by Norman Kings who were stocking their Sicilian pleasure parks with this species.[2] Whilst the role of the park as a source of venison should not be forgotten, it should be borne in mind that the medieval park was a multi-functional resource that served to keep people out (as well as animals in), and was also a very visible display of social status, both to the local community and the visitor. Depending upon resources within the park, the exploitation of minerals and timber may also have made a useful contribution to the cost of its upkeep or the more general economy of the manorial estate. In *Designs Upon the Land*, Oliver Creighton points out that the medieval park is solely referred to as 'parcus' in contemporary documents rather than as a deer park.[3] This perhaps reflects an acknowledgment at the time of the varied role of the park in the landscape.

A park did not necessarily exist in isolation, it may have been one of two or more in the same ownership, often closely adjacent to one another. These might fulfill separate and distinct roles in the immediate landscape. Powerful lords and the nobility often had parks associated with each of their geographically dispersed residences. For example, by the mid-sixteenth century, the De Vere family, Earls of Oxford had three separate parks abutting the castle at Hedingham (Great, Castle and Little Parks) as well as separate parks in the Colne Valley and also associated with some of their other residencies outside of Essex. The majority of medieval parks existed as a single feature in the landscape but even here the role of the park in re-enforcing the social status of its owner should not be underestimated.

Research over the past twenty years has also increased our understanding of the role of the medieval park in providing a setting or backdrop to the principal residence. A Little Park, where present, often contained symbols of seigneurial status such as dovehouses, water features and sometimes enclosed gardens within the park. They were thus especially important in fulfilling the role of enhancing the residence within the landscape. A Little Park always seems to have occurred in conjunction with at least one other larger adjacent park that was also in the same ownership. Despite the term 'Little' Park, these were rarely a diminutive feature in the landscape. For example, the Little Park at Thaxted covered an area of some one hundred and sixty acres. This park was held by the de Clare family who also held the Great Park (also known as Southfrithe) comprising six hundred and seventy one acres and Oldefrith, with one hundred and seventy nine acres in the same parish. Several examples of these early designed landscapes within 'Little Parks' can be found in Essex – at Hedingham (Castle Park), Pleshey, Thaxted, Great Bardfield and Little Easton – all of which had Little Parks surrounding or close to, a principal residence. There are more examples of these elite landscapes yet to be found.

Animals stocked within a park were not only a resource for the table; they were also rich with symbolism – both religious and as a reference to social status. All aspects of the hunt, the kill, and the distribution and consumption of the resulting meat were mediated through the status and hierarchy of the participants. For example, only the red and fallow deer were considered to be worthy of hunting and were considered 'noble' quarry to be pursued primarily by the nobility who were themselves termed 'gentle' hunters; the roe deer was classed as a 'rascal' or 'venery', along with the fox and marten and not worthy of pursuit. The red deer stag in particular had strong Christian associations and ritual significance and is often depicted in association with the crucified Christ in contemporary art. Such associations were not considered at all blasphemous in medieval society. Gaston Febus in his *Livre de Chasse* reassured the fourteenth century reader that to the Church, hunting was an acceptable pastime. He argued that those that hunted had a better appreciation of nature, and were thus happier than those that did not hunt, and hunters were therefore guaranteed a place in paradise in the afterlife.[4]

Braxted Park, Great Braxted (Essex)

Location, Soils and Topography

Braxted Park lies in the central western part of the parish of Great Braxted, Essex. The nearest town Witham, lies some 2 miles to the south west; Maldon on the mouth of the River Blackwater is approximately 4.5 miles due south as the crow flies. The underlying solid geology of Essex is of chalk which in the area of the Braxted Park estate is overlain by Kesgrave sands and gravels derived from the former course of the Thames. Soils on the estate are variable, but predominantly light loams of the Efford 2 series, with lenses of heavier Windsor series clays. The topography of the estate is gently undulating with higher ground to the eastern side of the park. The principal residence, Braxted Park House, sits more or less in the centre of the park on a prominence above the lakes at 40m above Ordnance Datum.

Archive Sources

Research on the medieval history of the park at Great Braxted has focused on the calendared rolls of central government and incidences of park break which give some insight into its early history. It is not until the late seventeenth century that a better understanding of the extent and management of the park has been possible. This is when leases, estate plans and other documents held in the Essex Record Office (ERO) provide more detailed information.

The period between 1751 when Peter Du Cane purchased the estate, and his death in 1803, is the best documented with a series of meticulously entered accounts and ledgers held in the ERO.[5] Subsequent accounts that were kept by Peter Du Cane's successors are less detailed, but still provide some understanding of the management of the park. Unfortunately, little descriptive

text about the park and its management has so far been discovered. The information available from the accounts has been extrapolated and expanded upon, and augmented with published information on deer park management to give an idea of the role of the deer in the landscape at Braxted Park.

Thirteenth – Fifteenth Century

The first securely documented reference to a park at Braxted occurs in 1342 when an incidence of park break and stealing of deer belonging to Mary de Sancto Paulo, Countess of Pembroke (second wife of Aymer de Valence) is recorded. The Countess of Pembroke's will of 1377 refers to the 'park with deer'. Although no specific mention of type of deer is mentioned it is likely that they would have been fallow deer which temperamentally were better suited to life in an enclosed space than the strongly territorial red deer. Writing in 1616, Gervase Markham points out that:

> 'You shall not by any means in one parke mix the red deere and the fallow deere together, for the red deere is a masterful beast, and when the time of bellowing cometh, he growes fierce and outrageous, ...and will kill the fallow deere...and therefore each must be kept severally in severall parkes'[6]

An ancestor of Aymer de Valence, William de Montchensy, made a warren at Great Braxted which is recorded in 1289. A contemporary or subsequent park may have incorporated a warren and the exact location of the park of the Countess of Pembroke is not known. However, it is suggested that the park and the warren were two distinct features in the landscape as an albeit much later plan dated 1778 by Matthew Hall Jnr., identifies the probable site of the warren as fifty-nine acres lying in six abutting fields outside of the then park. The six fields all had warren in their name – Hilly Warren, Old Barn Warren, Gravel Pit Warren, Park Gate Warren, The Middle Warren and Lea Lane Warren. This land lay to the south of the known extent of the eighteenth century park and is also probably the same land referred to in a lease of 1695 as 'the old warren ... about 66 acres' recorded as a separate feature to the park. These fields are also shown on the earlier plan of 1740.

After the death of the Countess of Pembroke in 1377, Braxted remained in the ownership of inter-linked branches of the de Valence family. By 1473 the estate was held by the de Greys of Ruthyn, Earls of Kent who, following on from a family feud, sold it to Sir Thomas Montgomery of Falkborne for 100 marks.

The Structure of the Park

To create an effective physical boundary which served to keep the animals within the park and restrict views into the elite landscape, the medieval park in the lowlands was most usually enclosed by the creation of a ditch and bank the latter being topped by a pale or fence. Ditches may have been up to six or seven feet deep and the pale was usually made of cleft oak, or sometimes a hedge was planted. Park pale fencing is often carefully illustrated on sixteenth and seventeenth century estate maps (*Figure 1*).

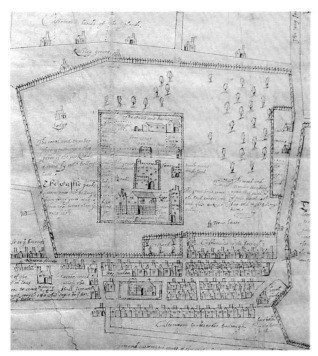

Figure 1 extract of plan of the Hedingham Castle Estate c.1650 showing the Castle Park enclosed by a wooden pale. (Reproduced courtesy of the Lindsey Family Hedingham Castle.)

From the mid-eighteenth century there are frequent references to mending the park pale at Braxted. For example, in 1751, James Browne (who undertook a considerable amount of work on the estate) was paid 10s. ½d for cleaving 350 pales, probably using estate timber although this is not stipulated.

Within the park pale a mosaic of habitats needed to be provided to accommodate deer (as can be seen on *Figure 2*, the 1740 plan of Braxted Park). The land included open grassland (grazing and hay and often referred to on plans as launds or lawns); individual trees and areas of thicker woodland (shelter and browse for parkland beasts and a source of timber and fuel) and a natural supply of water. Elm was a particularly important parkland tree as it is very palatable and the outer branches of pollard or single trees could be lopped either to provide immediate browse or the branches could be dried and stored for use in winter.

There is no documentary evidence to suggest the location for the choreographed Bow and Stable hunt that is the style most likely to have been practiced within a park.[7] However, the topography of the ground would suggest that in Braxted Park, a broad flat area of ground to the near north-east of the present house (and the probable site of the earlier hunting lodge) may have lent itself to the pursuit. This area is c.500 m in length and up to 200m in width.

Sixteenth and Seventeenth Centuries
Sir Thomas Montgomery did not stay at Braxted Lodge (as it was called at the time) for very long, and in 1509, it was sold to William Ayloffe of Hornchurch in whose family it was to stay for one hundred and one years until 1610.

The ownership of the estate in the mid to late seventeenth century is unclear with the account in Morant[8] not quite matching dates given in archived documents of the period. This is an area that would benefit from further detailed research. Sir Thomas Darcy, first Baron Darcy of Chiche (St. Osyth) is reputed to have purchased Braxted c.1650 for his eldest son, who proceeded to build a new residence on the site of the present day house. A letter of 1708, describes Braxted Lodge as a 'house not above 30 years old' however recent analysis (2009) of the brickwork by Andrew Derrick of the Architectural History Practice suggests that Darcy may have extended an existing building (possibly a hunting lodge) rather than starting to build afresh. The principal residence up until then had been situated to the immediate east of the Church: both buildings lying just outside of the boundary of the park (see *Figure 2*).

In 1695 Mrs Spratborough (who was the widow of William Spratborough, the park keeper for Thomas Darcy, and before him Sir John Cotton during the 1680s) leased part of Braxted Lodge and the park of 300 acres for a period of four years from Sir William Dawes of Lyons in Essex. The lease refers to:

> '... and also that that the park of deer and warren of conies belonging to the said ... containing by estimation 300 acres more or less together with free liberty of keeping feeding and killing deer and conies ... and also those several parcels of pasture ground commonly called the old warren and containing together about 66 acres...'

Sir William retained the right to fish and timber from the park. In addition, at the end of her tenure Mrs Spratborough was expected to leave the park stocked with 150 deer of varying ages including six mature bucks (deer were considered worthy of hunting once they had attained six years of age), eighteen four-year-old bucks, the remainder being younger animals.

In 1708, Mrs Windham of Felbrigg Hall in Norfolk hired Braxted Lodge: the lease describes the house as 'not above 30 years old' and the rental was £60 per year for six years. In letters to her son she describes it thus...

> '... A park stocked with deer, a river with ponds, warren, hay meadow, wood for my use and good gardens ...' April 26th 1708

and ...

> '.. a park of 300 acres, 200 deer, which I may kill as I please, stocked with plenty of rabbits, plenty of pheasants, woodcocks and game ... good ponds full of carp and perch and tench at command in stews...' May 1st 1708.

The Eighteenth and Nineteenth Centuries
In 1751 the Braxted estate was purchased by Peter Du Cane who had been made High Sheriff of Essex in 1745 and was to become a Director of the Bank of England between 1755 and 1783. He moved with his wife and family to Braxted Lodge which was by this time the principal residence. Du Cane paid £13,050 for the manor

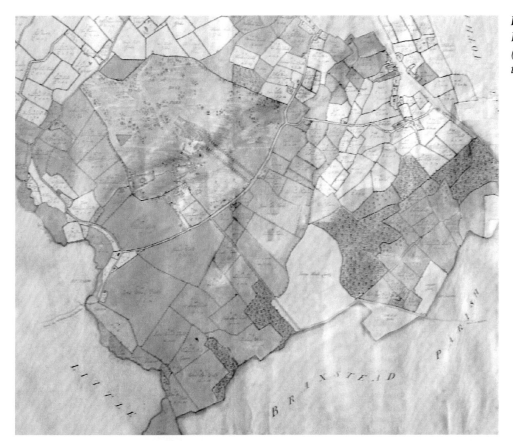

Figure 2 1740 *map of Braxted Park (detail). (Reproduced courtesy of the Braxted Park Estate.)*

of Great Braxted, the estate and five manor farms (a total of around 1500 acres). The timber and underwood were valued separately £997 9s 0d. The 44 ½ brace of deer in the park were valued at £119 14s. 0d. A further entry records that the cost of the deer is not being entered as a direct expense as 'being kept for pleasure I don't choose to value them'. This suggests that Peter Du Cane valued the deer for their amenity value as part of the backdrop to the new residence and also reminds us that by this period venison was available for purchase. It also perhaps reflects Du Cane's aspiration to move away from his merchanting background to become one of the foremost land owners in the county. Certainly, over the following ninety years Peter Du Cane and his successors invested in the house and landscape employing the architects Robert Taylor and later, John Johnson, to extend and alter the principal residence and service buildings. Within the park extensive planting was undertaken; the stew ponds amalgamated and enlarged to create ornamental lakes and additional land purchased to enable the park to be extended and enclosed with a brick wall, thus completing the transformation to a park which was considered in the 1920s to rank '...amongst the important residential seats in the county'.[9]

Peter Du Cane's accounts were sub divided into properties and other financial interests so it is reasonably straightforward to deduce items of income and expenditure relating to the park at Braxted. One of the earliest tasks was the mending of deer racks at a cost of 4s. 9d. which was undertaken by James Browne who was also paid for cleaving new park pales as mentioned above. Nine loads of hay had also been purchased. Fallow deer were generally considered not especially hardy and supplementary feeding of the deer and other livestock

was necessary in most parks during periods of drought and hard weather. During this period the park resources at Braxted were shared with 'Welch' [sic] cattle and sheep which were frequently bought and sold and this may account for the relatively low stocking density of deer. Robert Unwin, one of the tenant farmers in the 1750s, also paid an annual rental for the privilege of keeping his horse in the park. In *Some Account of English Deer Parks* Evelyn Shirley[10] comments that no more than one deer per acre was the usual stocking rate and that additional food in the form of hay, barley, wheat and beans should be provided especially in winter. The fruits of sweet chestnut, beech mast and acorns were also considered suitable. In 1753 at Braxted, two acres of park were ploughed to plant turnips for fodder.

Shirley advises that shelter is even more important to fallow deer than supplementary food and deduces that they must originate from warmer climes. The very dark or black fallow was reputed to be hardier than the spotted or lighter coated variety – Joseph Whitaker recorded that there were 100 black fallow stocked in the park at Wyvenhoe at the end of the nineteenth century.[11] A plan of Braxted Park in 1822 *(Figure 3)* shows a semi circular deer shelter to the southeast of the house. No record for the construction for this has been found in the accounts but it may well have been a fairly simple timber structure. It is thought that there are no surviving examples of deer shelters in Essex, nationally perhaps the best known is the mid-eighteenth century Gothic eye catcher built in the park of the Bishops of Durham at Bishop Auckland, although there are several other fine examples of stone and brick built shelters. The park keeper at Braxted is provided with a new coat and waistcoat each year and unusually, the washing of deer cloths

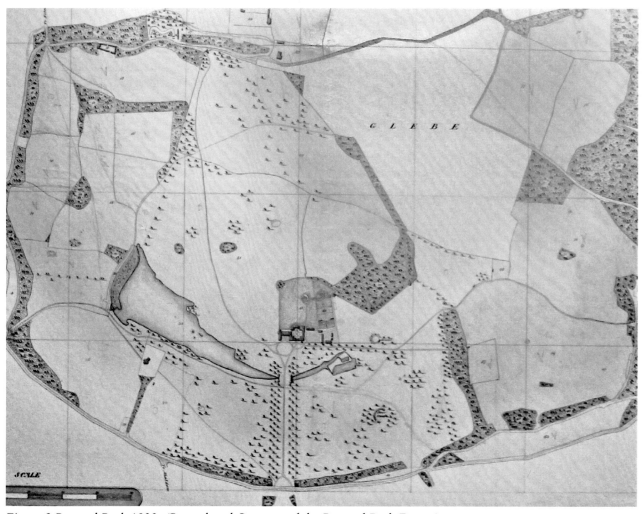

Figure 3 Braxted Park 1822. (Reproduced Courtesy of the Braxted Park Estate.)

is also recorded several times in the eighteenth century accounts. The author has found no other references to deer cloths and puts forward the suggestion that they may perhaps have been similar to a modern day horse blanket and were used to help to keep the deer warm?

A game or deer larder for the hanging of venison is the other building most likely to have been present in a park. Early examples would have been principally timber structures such as the fine example still extant at Rydal Hall in Cumbria. In Essex there are at least two examples of later more substantial brick dairy/game larders – at Down Hall (Hatfield Heath) and Trueloves (Brentwood). Both buildings are listed Grade II.

There are no records of exotic species of deer being introduced into the park at Braxted, although Peter Du Cane purchased four spotted Barbary sheep in June 1759. White's *Directory* of 1848 specifically mentions that 'the park has some fine specimens of Italian cattle' that had been introduced into the park by Charles Du Cane.[12] Elsewhere in Essex, by the late nineteenth century, the husbandry of a combined herd of red and fallow deer seems to have been mastered to some extent, as Whitaker records a herd of four hundred and fifty fallow and one hundred and twenty red deer at Easton; fifty fallow and forty red at Thorndon whilst at Weald, nine Sika or Japanese deer were being kept alongside both red and fallow.[13]

At Braxted the deer herd continued to be maintained and indeed increased in number, perhaps facilitated by the purchase of additional land. During his tenure between 1803 and 1823, Peter Du Cane II enlarged the park by purchasing around eighty acres of land on the western boundary of the 'Old' Park. Here, existing field boundaries were strengthened with additional planting to screen and enclose the parkland landscape and the northern approach was moved to the far side of the recently created main lake. A further forty acres comprising a gentleman's residence known as Fabians or, Faulkbournes with a small designed landscape (*Figure 3*) to the immediate north of the 'Old' park was purchased in 1812 but not incorporated into the park until after 1823. The expansion of the park was completed by Peter Du Cane III with a further purchase of land to the north east and the removal of houses and cottages close to the Church; enabling the building to be incorporated into the visual landscape of the park which now extended to five hundred acres. In 1825 work began on building the four and a half mile, red-brick, wall enclosing the park and three lodge cottages marking two of the principal entrances. Within the park a considerable amount of planting of individual trees and small plantations was undertaken to augment the existing avenues and planting. The 1838 Tithe Apportionment survey for the Parish shows that all but seventeen acres of land inside the park at this time was pasture.[14]

The Du Cane's occasionally sold venison, for example half a buck was sold to Mr. Strutt for £3 3s. 0d in August 1800. Between 1861 and 1868 there are records of one hundred and six does and seventy-two bucks being killed out of the park and Braxted is included in Shirley's account of deer parks published in 1867.[15] It is probable that the 1868 record is the end of the herd, as in the following year Charles Du Cane II and his family moved to Tasmania where he served as Governor for a period of five years.

Conclusion

The will of the Countess of Pembroke confirms that deer were present in the park at Braxted in 1377, and it is fair to speculate that this was the beginning of five hundred years of continuous history of deer in the park at Braxted. Although it cannot be established with certainty, it is probable that the park stood on the same site as the 'Old' park shown on the plan of 1740. Up until the late seventeenth century, the principal residence at Great Braxted was situated immediately alongside the twelfth century Church of All Saints, just outside of the park boundary. Dovehouse Field close to this main house, a warren, and stew ponds all suggest the presence of a high status landscape. The park was subsequently enlarged in the early nineteenth century by successive members of the Du Cane family. Comparison of documentary evidence from the late seventeenth and mid eighteenth centuries demonstrates the changing view point of the day. In the late seventeenth century, Mrs. Spratborough and Mrs. Windham clearly saw the deer in the park as a source of meat, whereas Peter Du Cane I viewed the animals as an integral part of the amenity of his new estate. Whilst many parkland herds of deer began to be disbanded in the seventeenth century in favour of cattle (which were considered to be more productive), the herd at Braxted continued to thrive. The last record for the deer in 1868 perhaps reflects the disbanding of the herd just prior to Charles Du Cane II emigrating in 1869. The estate was let during the absence of the family and the cost of the upkeep of the deer might not be looked upon favourably by any tenant.

Braxted Park is unusual in that it is one of only *circa* ten parks in Essex that successfully made the transition from medieval deer park to a fine example of a landscape park. The quality of Braxted Park as a landscape park is reflected in its grading as II* in the English Heritage Register of Parks and Gardens of Special Historic Interest. It is now the home of the Clark family who have lived there for nearly sixty years. An extensive programme of landscape restoration within the park began some ten years ago and as part of this, cattle and sheep have been re-introduced. However, any deer in the park today are part of the ubiquitous wild population in the county!

The author would like to thank Braxted Park Estate for their help with research into the history of the estate.

Bibliography

Almond, R., 2003 *Medieval Hunting*, Sutton Publishing

Calendar of Patent Rolls Edward III October 1342

Calendar of Inquisition Post Mortem 51 Edward III, 20th April 1377

Creighton, O., 2009 *Designs Upon the Land*, The Boydell Press

Cummins, J., 2005 *The Art of Medieval Hunting: The Hound and the Hawk*, Palgrave Macmillan

English Heritage Listed Buildings Online Register http://lbonline.english-heritage.org.uk accessed January 10th 2010

Gimson, W.A., 1958 *Great Braxted 1086-1957*, Tindal Press

Grant, J. (ed), c.1925 *Essex Historical, Biographical and Pictorial*, London & Provincial Publishing

Hunter, J. & Rackham, O., 2003 Essex Parks pre 1600, an unpublished gazetteer

Liddiard, R. (ed), 2007 *Medieval Parks: New Perspectives*, Windgather Press

Morant, P., 1768 *The History and Antiquities of the County of Essex*, London

Pattison, P. (ed), 1998 *There by Design: Field Archaeology in Parks and Gardens*, BAR Series 267

Shirley, E.P., 1867 *Some Account of English Deer Parks, with notes on the management of Deer*, (reprinted by Grimsay Press 2007)

Taylor, C., 2000 *Medieval Ornamental Landscapes*, i, 38-55

Wells, F., 2004 The Little Park in Essex 1100-1600, unpublished MA Thesis University of East Anglia

Whitaker, J., 1892 *A Descriptive List of the Deer Parks and Paddocks of England*, Ballantyne Hanson & Co

White, T., 1848 *Directory of Essex*, Great Braxted.

Archives

ERO – Essex Record Office

ERO D/DAc 43. Clayton MSS. 1630.

ERO D/DM T92. Mildmay Family Deeds 1621-1637.

ERO D/DU 19/26 Reference Table by Matthew Hall to map of Great Braxted

ERO D/DHt T38/7. Deeds of Great Braxted. 1695

ERO D/DHt T38/6 Deeds of Great Braxted December 1682.

ERO Q/SR 453/59 Court Session Rolls 1687.

ERO. D/DDc A12 Du Cane Family Accounts Ledger. 1750 – 1753 ff 86.

ERO D/DDc A15 Du Cane Family Accounts Ledger 1759 – 1762

ERO D/DDc A27 Du Cane Family Accounts Ledger 1799 – 1803 ff.98

ERO. D/DU 19/63 Manor of Kelvedon Hall in Great Braxted and Kelvedon. 1812 – 1860.

ERO D/CT 48A Great Braxted Tithe Award 1838.

Maps

The Lordship and Parish of Great Braxted. Surveyor Unknown. c.1740. Scale 16 inches to one mile. The Braxted Park Estate. Reduced photograph of map held at ERO T/M 415/1.

Great Braxted Park and other lands. Survey'd for E: Wakefield by W: Craggs. 1822. Scale: 20 in. to 1 mile The Braxted Park Estate. Reduced photograph of map held at ERO T/M 423/1.

References

1   Hunter & Rackham c.2003
2   Zoo-archaeological evidence has demonstrated that the Romano-British had consumed fallow which it seemed, had subsequently died out in England
3   Creighton 2009
4   For detailed descriptions of hunting and the ritual associated with it, the reader is directed to *Medieval Hunting* by Richard Almond and *The Hound and the Hawk* by J. Cummins
5   Du Cane records in the National Archive relate to their estates in London and Surrey so have not been relevant to Braxted Park.
6   In Essex, specific 'Red Deer' parks are recorded in the early 17th century at New Hall, Boreham and Woodham Walter.
7   see Almond 2003 and Cummins 2005
8   Morant 1768, ii, 137-140
9   Grant c.1925
10   Shirley 1867
11   Whitaker 1892
12   White 1848
13   Whitaker 1892
14   ERO D/CT 48B
15   Shirley 1867

Seen but not Herd: Essex Deer Parks in the Calendar of Patent Rolls 1232-1432, and Charter Rolls 1227-1516

Twigs Way
25 Elfleda Rd Cambridge CB5 8LZ

Introduction

During the twelfth to sixteenth centuries deer parks were one of the most widespread forms of landscape 'design'. Alongside warrens, fish (or stew) ponds, and dovecotes they incorporated elements of subsistence, status and aesthetics. At various times in the medieval and Early Modern period all these components of the manorial landscape required not only money for their construction and maintenance, but also specific permissions or licences for their creation and stocking, all of which reinforced their status. Deer parks in particular were the focus of a raft of legislation and less formal social regulation relating not only to the park itself, but the form of the boundary (the park pale), the presence of a deer leap, the process of obtaining the deer to stock it, and any hunting activities relating to the park and the surrounding landscape. This complex web of regulation and management resulted in deer parks appearing in a broad range of written records from personal accounts and letters, through manorial records, Quarter Sessions up to crown courts. Criminal activities focussed on the park, such as park breaks, poaching or trespass, were also subject to investigation and record at many levels. The court at which any crime might appear was partly dependant on the severity of the crime, but also on the status of the owner of the park or the perpetrator of the crime. Small scale trespass of the local lord's park might appear at a manorial court whilst a full scale park break by a mob led by the neighbouring gentry could merit an inquisition at the short lived Star Chamber (see Way 1997a for analysis).[1]

Research into particular deer parks, or parks within a specific county will often utilise the records of the local or county-based source materials. Manorial accounts listing costs of maintenance of the park pale, coppicing details within the park, or (more rarely) the exchange of deer or venison will give an insight into the workings of the park. Local courts will provide information on certain types of trespass, poaching or other park-focussed crimes, such as illegal continuation of gathering of undergrowth or timber following park creation and those crimes that are considered more serious will appear at the periodic courts of the Quarter Sessions[2] or Courts of Assize, still county based. Largely missing from these sources will be day-to-day records relating to royal parks (including granting of keepership or custody), granting of royal prerogatives such as the licences to impark,[3] grants of fines associated with the park, or park-focussed crimes of a serious nature or relating to royal parks.[4]

Information on these parks and events may instead appear in the royal letters and charters, the latter often associated with an appeal for royal notice.

This further 'level' of source material, issuing from the crown governance, not only provides a supplementary source of evidence for individual parks, but also allows us to gain an overview of parks at national and county level, enabling some assessment of the overall frequency of events such as park breaks, as well as an insight into the complex social relations formed by the continual grants and re-grants of licences, custodies and grants. It would be rare (although not unheard of) for a park to be 'discovered' within the Crown letters and records that had not already been noted by researchers and historians within the more local records, but in many cases further information can be gained on the history of specific parks in addition to the county-wide overviews and analysis. In other instances discovery of further information about a park within these national records may trigger research at the local level if it has not yet been undertaken

Background to the Present Article

As part of a doctoral project on the parks of Cambridgeshire, the present author undertook a national study of the Calendared records of both the Letters Patent (royal letters issued as 'open') and the Charter Rolls, the first for the period 1232-1432, and the latter for the period 1227-1516.[5] The study extracted from the Calendar of Letters Patent every record that included mention of a deer park, and from the Calendar of the Charter Rolls every record of a licence or grant to impark or enlarge a deer park, or otherwise alter the boundary (for example by creation of a deer leap).[6] The study incorporated all the counties of England and some references to Welsh material. The choice to concentrate on these particular records was based on the appearance in these of the licences to impark. Other forms of royal letters and records, including the Close Rolls (royal letters issued 'closed'), Fine Rolls (of financial 'offerings' to the crown), and Inquisitions Post Mortem (IPM) are also known to include reference to park business, but rarely to imparkment, which was the focus of the original study.

In each instance of a park being referred to in the Patent Rolls the study recorded the date of the record, the name of the park, where possible the modern name and location of the site, and the type of business or activity recorded. Categories of activity included Park Breaks, Trespass, Orders, Appointments of Keepership, Grants (of deer, or of pasture), Licences, Charters and 'Other'. 'Other' included oddities such as the reference to a chapel within the park bounds,[7] felling of trees within a park, impounding of cattle within parks,[8] surveying of royal parks,[9] and records of the keeping of warrens within parks,[10] amongst other things. The Charter Rolls, recording as they do specific charters issued through the Chancery, were more select in their references and concentrated on the granting of a charter to create or enlarge a park.

In the original study (published in 1997)[11] this wealth of information from a wide geographical and chronological spread, was then utilised to create a context against which to assess various social and cultural aspects of Cambridgeshire parks. The published research however also retained the tables of information created by the analysis of the Calendared material in the hope that it would prove of use to researchers in other counties or with research topics which might utilise the material. Subsequently the author has undertaken some other work based on the research, most notably on the social pattern and incidences of park-focussed crime in the thirteenth to sixteenth centuries[12] and references to the work in other publications indicate that use has been made of the tables by other researchers.[13]

Previous Work on Deer Parks in Essex

Substantial previous work has been carried out on Essex deer parks both at the county level and of individual parks.

Cantor's *Gazetteer*, published in 1983,[14] included Essex parks, as did the earlier writers on deer parks in England, most notably Shirley whose seminal 1867 publication[15] was based on a wide range of source materials. More recently John Hunter included research on deer parks in his publications on the landscape and field systems of Essex.[16] Parks were also considered within the publication of the 1996 Cressing Conference on *The Essex Landscape: In Search of its History*.[17] Detailed studies of individual parks have included that on Castle Hedingham (by Rob Liddiard and Fiona Wells)[18] and Fiona Wells' current work on Braxted Park in this publication

Whilst it is realised that the current publication of the references in the Patent Rolls and Charter Rolls may not add anything to these sites which have already been studied intensively, the information will hopefully add material to sites which have been little studied, and allow further research and assessment at a county level of patterns of park creation and enlargement, and activities such as park break, awarding of rights and offices etc in royal and aristocratic parks.

Discussion of Essex Deer Parks in the Calendar of Patent Rolls 1232-1432, and Charter Rolls 1227-1516 *(See Tables 1, 2 and 3)*.

The purpose of this article is the provision and circulation of the available information rather than any in depth analysis. However there are several points of interest which may usefully be highlighted from the listing of references to Essex parks.

The frequency of references to Essex parks:
Between 1232 and 1432 there are 256 references to matters arising in connection with Essex parks in the Calendar of Patent Rolls (not including licences to impark or enlarge existing parks, which accounted for a further 31) *(see Tables 1 and 2)*. Given the very specific concerns of the Patent Rolls with matters affecting the Crown governance this indicates the substantial social role and importance of the Essex parks. Although many of the instances relate to royal parks (such as Havering atte Bower) or parks in the vicinity of the Royal Forest, others have come to the attention of the crown governance through the nature of the business (for example serious park breaks).

The range of subjects and activities evidenced:
Obviously the range of activities and subjects are dictated and circumscribed by the 'jurisdiction' of the Patent Rolls. However within this there are still a considerable numbers of subjects covered, enabling us to build a picture of the activities associated with the ownership and management of a park. These include:

  licensing of parks,
  licensing of park enlargements,
  granting of the offices of keeper, bailiwick, clerk of works as necessary etc,
  custody of the park,
  enclosure with fencing, pales, walls and dykes,
  repairs to fencing, pales, walls and dykes (and responsibility for these),
  stocking the park (with deer),
  granting of various rights including agistment, estovers, pannage, herbage, browsing, brushwood, pasturage, keeping of animals, felling of wood,
  re-arrangement of tithes for imparked land,
  sale of underwood, timber, pasturage, herbage etc,
  granting of game and venison from the park,
  enquiry into park breaks and trespasses.

Although not all of these subjects will be covered for all parks, with details of management only being documented for the royal parks, this gives an insight into the constant management and upkeep of parks in this early period and can add considerably to our knowledge of specific parks. The management of Havering atte Bower for example is well documented as are Hadleigh and Rayleigh (all Crown parks).

Certain types of entry predominate for non-Crown parks, most especially licences, and enlargements (see below) and 'park breaks'.

For some parks the only evidence we have for their existence in the crown records is a complaint of park break. For example the park at Thorrington, (Cal Pat 23 January 1343, record of park break), Wakes Colne (Cal Pat 7 December 1325) and Wyles (Cal Pat 22 May 1309) (location unknown). Although detailed local research may result in further information it is this vital entry in the national records that may itself instigate local research. The uncertain role of licensing is also highlighted by the fact that none of the parks mentioned above have a surviving record of licensing despite being obviously in existence and the owners being confident in drawing attention to their park.

Parks not previously listed in published research are presented below (*Table 1*).

Table 1: Parks not encountered in previously published research.

Park	Earliest reference provided by present research	Comment
Great Horkesley (near Colchester)		
Layer de Hatley/ Lyre (probably Layer Bretton also known as Layer Marney)	1264	Impark
Low Leyton (varients Laindon /Leyndon)	1253	Impark Grove
Ongar (could be either Chipping/High)	21 June 1244	
Thriftwood/ Wraft (location unknown)	9 Nov 1296	Park Breaks
White Hall, Dunton		
Wyles (location unknown)	22 May 1309	Park Breaks

Notes:
Identification can be problematical where various spelling/names are used: In addition several entries indexed as Essex in the Calendar of Patent Rolls are not in fact in Essex, these have been omitted where realised.

Initial creation and enlargement of parks

Theoretically the creation or enlargement of any park required a licence (purchased for an often considerable amount) which was documented either in the Patent Rolls or the Charter Rolls, or very occasionally the Close Rolls. The compliance with the requirement to licence and the strictness with which the licence was enforced varied over time (perhaps in relation to the state of the royal coffers) but has been argued as being most strict for those in the vicinity of a royal park or the royal forests. Not all licences resulted in a park being created, the licence itself being seen as a proof of status and royal favour. Some parks were never licensed or were licensed retrospectively (see Way 1997b for discussion), but the record of licences does give a starting point for an exploration of park creation and enlargement in Essex. It also highlights some anomalies in licensing with some parks being supposedly licensed after they had already been noted in connection with other activities. This is an area where further research might be carried out comparing the research already carried out by John Hunter and Fiona Wells into local records with the results of the present research.

New Information on Creation etc of Essex Parks

Although it might have been thought that the work of previous researchers in the national records (most especially Cantor)[19] would have resulted in a 'earliest dates' for all Essex parks having been established by now, a rapid comparison of dates for the first mention of parks in *Tables 3, 4, and 5* and the lists produced by Hunter and Wells based on Cantor, produces some new material on these 'earliest dates' as presented below (*Table 2*).

Table 2: Previously published 'earliest dates' for parks, now given an earlier date

Park	Previous earliest date	Earliest date provided by present research
Absoll Park/ Apechilde/ Applechilde (Great Waltham)	1449	1 December 1347 (and further on 26 May 1376)
Horsfrith (possibly an outling part of Writtle Forest)	1284	7 June 1280
Little Leighs	Map of 1609	10 March 1380
Purleigh	1296	25 Feb 1228
Ramsden (Bellhouse?)	uncertain reference in 1291	12 July 1421 firm reference to a park
Thundersley (NB there may be some confusion beteen Thundersley and Thunderley)	1416	27 May 1366 (and subsequent)
Weald (poss. North Weald Bassett or South Weald)	no date	24 July 1260
Weald (in South Weald?)	no date	1 September 1295

Notes:
Absol was part of the complex of parks which included Absol, Littley, Pleshey Little Park and Pleshey Great Park (see Table 3).[20]

Horsfrith was probably an outlying part of Writtle Forest (cf Rackham) south of the road between Ongar and Chelmsford. Reaney's *The Place-Names of Essex* (CUP 1935) lists Horsefrithpark Wood in Writtle parish - parco de Horsfrithe in 1429 - and has no other entries for Horsefrith under other parishes.[21]

Park Breaks

Although, as has been indicated, the Crown records are biased toward Crown-owned land (or land adjoining such), or certain actions and events, one can still use the records to look for patterns of events. Most particularly, the incidence of park break, or more accurately the incidence of reporting of park break to the Crown.

Although the current research has only examined the period 1232-1432 for the Patent Rolls within this period there are clear patterns. Park breaks appear comparatively rarely until the last part of the thirteenth century, then gain slowly in numbers until the end of the century when there is a substantial rise in numbers, in particular in the period from 1300-1330. They then decline again rapidly. This pattern is substantially the same as that noted for the rest of the country in previous studies, although possibly a little earlier.[22] It is notable that the peak of reporting is not at the period of the Black Death (1348-1350) or in the subsequent social upheaval that followed, but predates that. The increase in park breaks may instead be a reflection of the sheep and cattle murrains of the earlier fourteenth century, which combined with poor weather and crop failures resulted in the widespread famines of 1315-17. In order to clarify the relationship between the famines, (which predominantly affected the poorer and middling classes) and the park breaks, an analysis would need to be undertaken of which classes of people were involved in the crime and the exact nature. For example whether deer were poached during the break, or whether the break was an assault instead on the pale, a representation of lordship. If the park breaks were carried out by gentry and landed classes then one could suppose either that the famines were more wide reaching in their direct effect on ability to procure foodstuffs (for example if gentry were involved in removing game), or if the focus was the park itself (a statement of status), that the famines had triggered a wider social unrest. Notable exceptions to the general pattern might indicate particular local circumstances, such as a direct response to recent imparkment or enlargement or local unrest. The publication of the lists of entries in the Crown records will hopefully facilitate exactly this type of research.

Type and Quality of Land Imparked:

Previous studies of parks at county level have argued variously that parkland was created either on poor or distant ground within the locality,[23] or on 'average' ground when assessed against the rest of the land available. To carry out such an assessment necessitates identifying which land was 'available' for the land-owner creating the park, locating the area that the park was created on, and then utilising modern agricultural evaluations of the land/geology of those areas to establish whether the land occupied by the park was of lesser/ identical/ better land than available. Such studies are time-consuming and best carried out at the local level for individual sites or groups of sites which can then be combined.

However at a very general level some assessment can be made of the type of land, or more particularly the *previous usage* of land that was imparked, by examination of the licences to impark and enlarge. Again this is not the place for detailed analysis, but a brief overview suggests the following:

Licences to impark or enlarge prior to c1310 appear to concentrate on woodland (for example Horsfrith (7 June 1280) and Lyre or Layer (20 October 1264) and there are indications that these are typically small areas of 10-20 acres, although there are exceptions such as Waltham (le Pleso) with 150 acres of demesne enclosed. After the middle of the fourteenth century much larger areas are imparked and typically these include 'land' (usually understood to mean agricultural land), demesne land, lawns, meadow, pasture and even a 'perilous lane' at Harolds Park/Copped Hall (perhaps one of the first ever recorded road diversions for park creation) (Cal Pat.

1 August 1380). When viewed against the size of a parish or manorial demesne, removal of 100 acres (Little Leighs), 300 acres (White Hall, Dunton; Wickham; West Horndon) or 400 acres (Ingrave and Great Thorndon) of this utilisable land would have a substantial impact on the local economy and social relations even in a period when population levels were low following the Black Death. Although the current study did not continue into the sixteenth century, when population levels and land pressure were again rising, studies in other areas have established that imparment of large areas of productive land continued into these periods often peaking in the sixteenth century.[24]

Conclusion

Drawing on earlier research into the Patent Rolls and Charter Rolls of crown governance, this article has demonstrated that there is considerable information to be gained concerning Essex parks from these records. Particular areas of future research have been highlighted, including: incorporating new information on park creation with existing work; location of previously unknown parks; incorporating and analysing new information on the management and economies of Crown-owned parks in particular; detailed investigation and analysis of the reports of park breaks; and analysis of the type and quality of land imparked with assessment of change over time; all to be set within the context of other social and economic changes. Some initial analysis of the information contained in these fascinating records indicate that medieval and Early Modern Essex deer parks may have a vital role to play in our understanding of economic and social relations in the local, regional and national context. With recent research on medieval parks in other counties now becoming available (notably the 2009 publication of *Medieval Parks of Hertfordshire*),[25] and renewed interest in status landscapes of the Middle Ages,[26] the time has come for a substantial and detailed research project focussing on Essex parks following in the footsteps of John Hunter. Hopefully this article is a small step on the way.

Bibliography

Andrews, D and P Ryan, 1999 'The 16th and 17th centuries: manors, mansions, parks and fields' In L.S. Green (1999) *The Essex Landscape: In Search of its History* Essex County Council pp40-50

Cantor, L., 1983 *The Medieval Deer Parks of England: A Gazetteer*, Loughborough University.

Creighton, O., 2009 *Designs upon the Land: Elite Landscapes of the Middle Ages*, Boydell Press.

Hoppitt, R., 1992 Medieval Deer Parks of Suffolk, unpublished PhD for University of East Anglia.

Hunter, J., 1999 *The Essex Landscape: A Study of its Form and History*, Essex Record Office

Hunter, J., 2003 *Field Systems in Essex*, Essex Society for Archaeology & History Occasional Paper (new series) no: 1

Liddiard, R., & Wells, F., 2008 'The Little Park at Castle Hedingham: A Possible Late Medieval Pleasure

Ground' in *Garden History*, 36, i, 85-93

Reaney, P. H.,1935 *The Place-Names of Essex* CUP 1935

Rowe, A., 2009 *Medieval Parks of Hertfordshire*, University of Hertfordshire Press

Shirley, E.P., 1867 *Some Account of English Deer Parks*, John Murray

Way, T., 1997a 'The Victim or the Crime: Park Focussed Conflict in Cambridgeshire and Huntingdonshire 1200-1556' in Carmen, J., (ed) *Material Harm: archaeological studies in war and violence*, Cruithne Press, 143-166

Way, T, 1997b *A Study of the Impact of Imparkment on the Social Landscape of Cambridgeshire and Huntingdonshire from c1080-1760*, BAR British Series 258

References

1 Way 1997 a,143-166

2 The Courts of Quarter Sessions were periodic courts held in each county and county borough in England and Wales until 1972, when they were abolished together with the Courts of Assize (Assizes). The Quarter Sessions generally heard crimes which could not be tried summarily by the local justices of the peace without a jury in petty sessions, which were sent up by the process of indictment to be heard in Quarter Sessions. The Quarter Sessions in each county were made up of two or more justice of the peace, presided over by a chairman, who sat with a jury. The Quarter Sessions did not have jurisdiction to hear the most serious crimes, most notably those which could be punished by capital punishment. These crimes were sent for trial at the periodic Assizes.

3 For a discussion of the rather variable requirement of a royal licence prior to the creation of a private park see Way 1997b

4 Some of these may appear in the local or county courts before working their way up to royal notice.

5 A previous study, by Cantor 1983, which listed the deer parks in each county of England and Wales, with the earliest mention of each, was found to have been based on the inadequate indexes of the official records, rather than a thorough search of the actual Calendars. (Cantor pers. comm.)

6 A 'deer leap' was a modification in the normal park pale such that deer could access the park from the outside, but once in would be trapped. Technically this meant that if the park was situated within or adjacent to an area of royal forest (a legal rather than landscape term) the owner would be acquiring royal deer. At certain periods it was argued that any deer were the property of the crown and thus even parks outside the very large areas designated as royal forest would also be liable for accusations of stealing royal deer if they inserted a deer leap.

7 Cal. Pat. 7 November 1343, Windsor, Berkshire

8 Cal.Pat. 30 January 1348 Radley, Berkshire, and others

9 Cal. Pat. 8 September 1354 Lubbesthorpe, Leicestershire, and others

10 Cal. Pat. 1 December 1360 Clipstone, Buckinghamshire, and others.

11 Way 1997b

12 Way 1997a, 143-166

13 The recent publication of Rowe 2009, for example

14 Cantor 1983

15 Shirley 1867

16 Hunter 1999 & 2003

17 Published as conference papers in 1999

18 Liddiard & Wells 2008, 85-93

19 Cantor 1983

20 I would like to thank Fiona Wells for this information.

21 I would like to thank Michael Leach for this, and other information about the location of some of these place names. Fiona Wells has also indicated that this is the location that herself and Rob Liddiard had confirmed for Horsfrith based on references in 1462.

22 Way 1997a & 1997b

23 Hoppitt 1992

24 Way 1997b

25 Way 1997b

26 Rowe 2009

27 Creighton 2009

Table 3: Park References within the Calendar of Patent Rolls 1232-1432

Date	Modern name	Ancient Name	Comments
1 December 1347	Absoll Park (Gt. Waltham)	Apechild	Licence to crenellate a manor lying in the park thereof
26 May 1376	Absoll Park (Gt. Waltham)	Apechilde Park	Grant of Bailiwick
15 November 1302	Aythorpe Roding? (could be Berners Roding)	Rothing	Park Break
12 March 1342	Baddow	Badewe	Park Break
10 November 1399	*Barnston*	*Bernestone*	*possible grant of parks (dubious)*
10 November 1399	Berners Roding	Rodyngberners	possible grant of parks *(dubious)*
1 June 1360	Blackley (loc. unknown)	Blaklegh	Park Break
14 July 1260	Bowers (loc. unknown)	Buris	Park Break
18 March 1299	Bramblety (loc. unknown)	Brembeltye	Park Break
2 July 1333	Bronneshoo (*Note: is this Broomeshawbury, Hatfield Broad Oak?*)	Bronesho	Park Break
14 November 1318	Clacton	Clacton	Park Break
10 November 1399	*Crippings*	*Cryppynges*	*possible grant of parks (dubious)*
28 June 1291	Cronden (in Stock)	Crunden	Park Break
2 November 1291	Cronden (in Stock)	Crunden	Park Break
29 October 1374	Crondon (in Stock)	Crondone	Grant of Office. Pasture for 3 oxen, 3 foals, pannage 4 swine, collect all agistments.
26 November 1386	Crondon (in Stock)	Croundon	Grant of office
14 November 1318	Crondon (in Stock)	Crundal	Park Break

Date	Modern name	Ancient Name	Comments
14 March 1301	Danbury	Daningebury	Park Break
26 July 1302	Danbury	Danygebury	Park Break
27 May 1401	Earls Colne	Earls Colne	Park Break
20 July 1314	Eastwood	Estewode	Park Break? possible was a free warren or chase
19 March 1310	Eastwood	Estwode	Confirmation Grant to Queen
1 February 1327	Eastwood	Estwode	Granted to Queen
20 July 1335	Eastwood	Estwode	Survey of Queens Parks
1 August 1352	Eastwood	Estwode	Mention of Park
10 December 1296	*Flaxham (no location known)*	*Flaxham*	*Park Breaks (dubious)*
30 March 1335	Gosfield	Gosefeld	Park Break including taking cattle
28 January 1314	Gosfield	Gosfeld	Park Break
22 April 1314	Gosfield	Gosfeld	Park Break
30 July 1403	Great Bardfield	Berdefeld	Office of parker
8 February 1406	Great Bardfield	Berdefelde	Park Break
20 May 1310	Great Bardfield	Berdefeld	Park Break
17 July 1316	Great Bardfield	Berdefeld	Park Break
1 June 1319	Great Bardfield	Berdefeld	Park Break
1 October 1342	Great Braxted	Braxsted	Park Break
5 July 1376	Great Braxted	Braxsted	Keeping of park
9 May 1303	Great Chesterford	Cestreford	Park Break
28 May 1317	Great Chesterford	Cestreford	Pasture in park and estovers
24 August 1384	Great Chesterford	Cestreford	Confirmation of custody
22 November 1399	Great Chesterford	Chesterford	Custody of Park
10 December 1366	Great Chesterford	Chestreford	Park Break
11 October 1390	Great Chesterford	Chestreford	Park Break
6 September 1340	Great Chesterford	Great Chasterford	Park Break
14 March 1356	Great Chesterford	Great Chesterford	Park Break
1 August 1405	Great Chesterford	Great Chesterford	Office of parker
10 September 1341	Great Dunmow	Dunmawe	Park Break
12 March 1342	Great Dunmow	Dunmawe	Park Break
17 February 1299	Great Hallingbury	Halingbury	Park Breaks
12 July 1421	Great Hallingbury	Halynbury	Mention of park
20 July 1314	Great Horkesley	Great Horkesle	Park Break? possible was a free warren or chase
28 October 1304	Great Waltham	Great Waltham	Park Break
12 March 1342	Great Waltham	Great Waltham	Park Break
26 May 1376	Great Waltham	Littlehay Park (Waltham)	Grant of Bailiwick
14 November 1296	Great Waltham	Great Waltham	Park Breaks
10 September 1341	Great Waltham	Great Waltham	Park Break
28 August 1283	Great Waltham	Great Waltham	Park Break
1 February 1327	Hadleigh	Haddeeye	Granted to Queen
20 February 1373	Hadleigh	Haddele	Wood felled in park
10 April 1377	Hadleigh	Haddele	Appt clerk of works
31 May 1377	Hadleigh	Haddele	Appt clerk of works
1 February 1378	Hadleigh	Haddele	Grant of custody
25 June 1379	Hadleigh	Haddele	Grant of office
20 April 1380	Hadleigh	Haddele	Sale of underwood
18 January 1381	Hadleigh	Haddele	Grant of park
3 October 1386	Hadleigh	Haddele	Clerk of works
13 July 1271	Hadleigh	Haddelegh	Park to be stocked with deer
27 May 1366	Hadleigh	Haddelegh	Repair hedges and enclosures in park
4 January 1375	Hadleigh	Haddelegh	Making a trench from the stank in the park to the lodge there.
1 August 1380	Hadleigh	Haddelegh	Grant of park with profit of herbage in return for finding proper sustenance for the deer
5 September 1311	Hadleigh	Haddeleye	Stud in park
27 November 1395	Hadleigh	Hadle	Grant of game and venison
20 October 1399	Hadleigh	Hadle	Office of parker
27 October 1399	Hadleigh	Hadle	Lodges in park
28 September 1255	Hadleigh	Hadlegh	Appointment [of keeper]

Date	Modern name	Ancient Name	Comments
10 October 1272	Hadleigh	Hadlegh	Grant to Queen
23 August 1273	Hadleigh	Hadlegh	Grant to Queen
27 October 1274	Hadleigh	Hadlegh	Grant to Queen
20 July 1314	Hadleigh	Hadlegh	Park Break? possible was a free warren or chase
30 July 1358	Hadleigh	Hadlegh	Appt keeper including herbage for horse and oxen
5 December 1372	Hadleigh	Hadlegh	Repair of enclosure in park
26 February 1385	Hadleigh	Hadlegh	Remove underwood to improve herbage
14 November 1409	Hadleigh	Hadlegh	Mention of park
22 August 1398	Hadleigh	Hadley	Grant to take venison in park
16 April 1305	Hadleigh	Hadleye	Park Break
19 March 1310	Hadleigh	Hadleye	Confirmation Grant to Queen
9 February 1391	Hadleigh	Hadleye	Mention of park
12 July 1421	Hatfield Broad Oak	Hatfield	Mention of park
2 Sept 1234	Hatfield Broad Oak	Hathfield	Grant of Custody
12 March 1342	Hatfield Broad Oak	Hatfield	Park Break
9 November 1264	Havering atte Bower	Havering	Park Keeping
13 October 1266	Havering atte Bower	Havering	Rent of Kings park and manor
13 September 1267	Havering atte Bower	Havering	'other'
23 August 1273	Havering atte Bower	Havering	Grant to Queen
27 October 1274	Havering atte Bower	Havering	Grant to Queen
20 October 1303	Havering atte Bower	Havering	Park Break
12 March 1307	Havering atte Bower	Havering	Park Break
10 October 1272	Havering atte Bower	Haveringes	Grant to Queen
5 March 1318	Havering atte Bower	Haveringg[es]	Given in Dowry
19 March 1310	Havering atte Bower	Haveringges	Confirmation Grant to Queen
20 July 1314	Havering atte Bower	Haveringges	Park Break? possible was a free warren or chase
16 April 1305	Havering atte Bower	Haveryng	Park Break
12 January 1331	Havering atte Bower	Haveryng	Appointment
1 January 1331	Havering atte Bower	Haveryng	Other (mention)
20 March 1381	Havering atte Bower	Haveryng	selling of underwood
19 February 1395	Havering atte Bower	Haveryng	Gift of 3 bucks a year
26 October 1397	Havering atte Bower	Haveryng	mention of park
25 February 1318	Havering atte Bower	Haveryng atte Boure	Custody Granted
10 September 1299	Havering atte Bower	Haverynge	Park Granted as Dowry
20 July 1335	Havering atte Bower	Haverynge	Survey of Queens Parks
5 March 1380	Havering atte Bower	Haverynge	Remission of duties to repair fence
1 May 1380	Havering atte Bower	Haverynge	Remission of repair of 467 perches of 18 feet each of paling and enclosure in return for rent of 5 marks yearly
30 March 1373	Havering atte Bower	Haveryng atte Boure	To at once enclose with palings as necessary
31 October 1399	Havering atte Bower	Haveryng	Grant of 3 bucks in park
19 February 1400	Havering atte Bower	Haveryng	Mention of park
8 September 1400	Havering atte Bower	Haveryng	Supervision of park
12 January 1339	Havering atte Bower	Haveryng atte Boure	Confirmation of grant of loppings after grass and after pannage of park
10 September 1348	Havering atte Bower	Haveryng atte Boure	Timber being used from the park
4 December 1352	Havering atte Bower	Haveryng atte Boure	Park Break
9 August 1354	Havering atte Bower	Haveryng atte Boure	Timber being used from the park
20 August 1355	Havering atte Bower	Haveryng atte Boure	Timber being used from the park
20 April 1357	Havering atte Bower	Haveryng atte Boure	Making enclosure of park
14 August 1369	Havering atte Bower	Haveryng atte Boure	Herbage for two mares in park
10 March 1371	Havering atte Bower	Haveryng atte Boure	Grant of stubs of oak in park
26 November 1376	Havering atte Bower	Haveryng atte Boure	Mention of Park
10 April 1377	Havering atte Bower	Haveryng atte Boure	Appt clerk of works
23 March 1378	Havering atte Bower	Haveryng atte Boure	Office of keeper
23 March 1378	Havering atte Bower	Haveryng atte Boure	Grant of keeping
5 March 1394	Havering atte Bower	Haveryng atte Boure	Agistment in park
5 November 1399	Havering atte Bower	Haveryng atte Boure	Custody with herbage and aftermath, pannage and after pannage, browsing and brushwood
28 June 1401	Havering atte Bower	Haveryng atte Boure	Custody with herbage, pannage, browsing, aftermath etc

Date	Modern name	Ancient Name	Comments
1 July 1413	Havering atte Bower	Haveryng atte Boure	Office Parker
1 February 1421	Havering atte Bower	Haveryng atte Boure	Office of parker
21 January 1331	Havering atte Bower	Haverynge atte Boure	Appointment/Grant
21 May 1323	Havering atte Bower	Haveryng atte Boure	Park Break
9 November 1296	Hide	Hyde	Park Breaks
28 August 1283	High Easter (& Gt Waltham)	High Estre	Park Break
14 November 1296	High Easter (& Gt Waltham)	High Estre	Park Breaks
12 March 1342	High Easter (& Gt Waltham)	Highestre	Park Break
26 May 1376	High Easter (& Gt Waltham)	Old Park High Estre	Grant of Bailiwick
20 May 1355	High Ongar	High Angre	Park Break (3 years before)
9 November 1296	Horsfrith (probably part of Writtle Forest)	Horsfrith	Park Breaks
26 September 1284	Horsfrith	Horsfrith	Stocking park by taking live bucks and does from the forest
28 June 1291	Langham	Langham	Park Break
10 September 1291	Langham	Langham	Park Break
nd March 1292	Langham	Langham	Trespass of Venison
1 August 1294	Langham	Langham	Park Break taking bucks and does
14 November 1409	Langley (Kings) (note: there is some query whether this is Langley In Essex or Kings Langley in Herts)	Chilternelangey	Mention of park
12 November 1279	Lawford	Lalleford	Park Break
28 July 1312	Lexden	Lexeden	Park Break
8 August 1312	Lexden	Lexeden	Park Break
6 July 1343	Lexden	Lexeden	Park Break
30 May 1347	Little Easton	Eyston	Park Break
8 August 1347	Little Easton	Eyston	Park Break
22 June 1411	Little Hallingbury	Little Halyngbury	Park break; Taken sorrel and doe, worth 10 marks, 2 fawns 5 marks, and trespass.
19 January 1278	Matching	Macching	Park Break including breaking gate of park
26 March 1320	Matching	Macchyng	Park Break
4 April 1320	Matching	Macchyng	Park Break
28 April 1314	Mountnessing	Gyng Mounteny	Park Break
6 June 1335	Nazeing	Nassing	Park Break
22 June 1373	Ongar	Angrepark (by le Golet)	Pardon for acquiring in fee
21 June 1244	Ongar	Aungre	Survey of Park
10 September 1341	Pleshey	Plesset	Park Break
12 March 1342	Pleshey	Plessy	Park Break
9 November 1296	Purleigh	Purlee	Park Breaks
12 July 1421	Ramsden Bellhouse	Ramesden	Mention of park
20 February 1373	Rayleigh	Raylegh and Hadlegh	Wood felled in park
27 November 1395	Rayleigh	Reilegh	Grant of game and venison
3 February 1300	Rayleigh	Reylegh Park	Pardon for taking of bucks, fawns and fawn of a hind
31 May 1377	Rayleigh	Raylee	Appt clerk of works
9 December 1377	Rayleigh	Raylee	Grant Office
3 October 1386	Rayleigh	Raylee	Clerk of works
20 July 1335	Rayleigh	Reilegh	Survey of Queens Parks
27 October 1399	Rayleigh	Reilegh	Lodges in park
14 November 1409	Rayleigh	Reilegh	Mention of park
9 February 1391	Rayleigh	Reileigh	Grant of profits of herbage
20 October 1303	Rayleigh	Relegh	Park Break
12 March 1307	Rayleigh	Releye	Park Break
19 March 1310	Rayleigh	Releye	Confirmation Grant to Queen
18 January 1381	Rayleigh	Reyle	Grant of park
22 August 1398	Rayleigh	Reyle	Grant to take venison in park
16 April 1305	Rayleigh	Reylee	Park Break
30 September 1295	Rayleigh	Reylegh	Custody of Park
20 July 1314	Rayleigh	Reylegh	Park Break? possible was a free warren or chase
1 March 1319	Rayleigh	Reylegh	Other. Kings Park in Stud
1 February 1327	Rayleigh	Reylegh	Granted to Queen

Date	Modern name	Ancient Name	Comments
1 August 1352	Rayleigh	Reylegh	Mention of Park
1 October 1361	Rayleigh	Reylegh	Pasture for 6 cows within park
27 May 1366	Rayleigh	Reylegh	Repair hedges and enclosures in park
25 June 1379	Rayleigh	Reylegh	Grant of office
20 April 1380	Rayleigh	Reylegh	Sale of underwood
1 August 1380	Rayleigh	Reylegh	Grant of park with profit of herbage in return for finding proper sustenance for the deer
20 June 1384	Rayleigh	Reylegh	Confirmation of pasturage for 6 cows
26 February 1385	Rayleigh	Reylegh	Remove underwood to improve herbage
27 June 1391	Rayleigh	Reylegh	Confirmation of keeper
22 July 1418	Rayleigh	Reylegh	Mention of park
20 July 1260	Rayleigh and Hadleigh	Raylegh and Hadlegh	Sale of wood in Rayleigh to repair Hadleigh
11 July 1248	Rettendon	Ratendon	New Enclosure of Park which had been enclosed with a wall, with dyke and hedge
12 May 1387	Rivenhall	Reunal	Custody during minority
8 August 1295	Rivenhall	Rowenhale	Park Break
1 August 1352	Rochford	Rcheford	Mention of park
12 March 1342	Saffron Walden	Walden	Park Break
17 November 1419	Saffron Walden	Walden	Keeper of park
14 November 1323	Saffron Walden	Waleden	Park Break
18 September 1314	Shenfield	Shenefeld	Park Break
1 April 1300	Stanford	Staneford	Licence to Demise
12 October 1298	Stanford Rivers	Stanford	Manor to let (with park?)
26 March 1320	Stanford Rivers	Stanford	Park Break
4 April 1320	Stanford Rivers	Stanford	Park Break
12 January 1328	Stanford Rivers	Stanford Ryvers	Park Break
18 September 1314	Stanley	Stanleye	Park Break
25 October 1283	Stanstead Mountfitchet	Stansted	Park Break
19 June 1258	Stapleford Tawney	Stapleford	Park Break
20 May 1310	Thaxted	Thakstede	Park Break
10 January 1324	Thaxted	Thakstede	Grant of Manor excluding the venison in the parks
8 April 1340	Theydon Gernon	Theydon Gernoun	Park Break
23 January 1343	Thorrington	Thoryngton	Park Break
9 November 1296	Thriftwood	Wraft	Park Breaks
5 December 1372	Thundersley	Thudresle	Sale of wood in park
27 May 1366	Thundersley	Thunderle	Repair hedges and enclosures in park
4 January 1375	Thundersley	Thunderle	Making a trench from the stank in the park to the lodge there.
25 June 1379	Thundersley	Thunderle	Grant of office
20 April 1380	Thundersley	Thunderle	Sale of underwood
18 January 1381	Thundersley	Thunderle	Grant of park
26 February 1385	Thundersley	Thunderle	Remove underwood to improve herbage
31 May 1377	Thundersley	Thunderlee	Appt clerk of works
3 October 1386	Thundersley	Thunderlee	Clerk of works
22 August 1398	Thundersley	Thunderlee	Grant to take venison in park
20 March 1381	Thundersley	Thunderlegh	Selling of underwood
27 November 1395	Thundersley	Thunderley	Grant of game and venison
20 October 1399	Thundersley	Thunderly	Office of parker
1 February 1377	Thundersley	Thundresle	Grant of park with repairs of wood, tithes to pay of 20s yearly for land acquired an enclosed in park
1 February 1378	Thundersley	Thundresle	Grant of park excepting venison
1 February 1378	Thundersley	Thundresle	Grant of custody
22 July 1418	Thundersley	Tunderle	Mention of park
27 October 1399	Thundersley	Tunderley	Lodges in park
7 December 1325	Wakes Colne	Colne Quency	Park Break
6 June 1335	Waltham	Waltham	Park Break
nd August 1271	Waltham (Harolds Park)	Wautham (Heraldsparc)	Park Break
1 December 1295	Weald	Weald	Park Breaks
22 May 1309	Weald	Welde	Park Break

Date	Modern name	Ancient Name	Comments
I September 1295	Weald	Waude	Park Breaks
I September 1295	Wix	Wykes	Park Break
I December 1295	Wix	Wykes	Park Breaks
14 May 1299	Wix	Wykes	Park Break
5 June 1299	Wix	Wykes	Park Break
12 March 1324	Wix	Wykes	Park Break
20 July 1260	Woodham	Wodeham	Park Break
17 February 1299	Woodham	Wodenham	Park Breaks
30 May 1362	Woodham Walter	Wodeham Wauter	Grant of Wood in park
11 September 1341	Writtle	Writele	Park Break
18 October 1374	Writtle	Writtele	Keeper of park
6 May 1378	Writtle	Writtele	Grant of park
19 June 1391	Writtle	Writtele	Keepership of park
16 April 1305	Writtle	Wrtleye	Park Break
12 July 1421	Writtle	Wrytell	Mention of park
22 May 1309	Wyles (location unknown)	Wyles	Park Break

Table 4: Licences to Impark or Enlarge Parks Contained within the Calendar of Patent Rolls 1232-1432

Date	Modern Name	Ancient name	Comments
16 June 1324	?	Baracheia and Rucheia	Impark woods to create a single park
16 July 1310	Aythorpe Roding	Eytrope Rothinge	Impark Wood
6 February 1292	Berners Roding	Rothing Berners	Licence to enlarge by adding 60 acres of own land
29 April 1286	Chignal, Tany, Writtle	Chigenhale, Tany, Wrytele	Impark grove of 14 acres and 6 acres of land to form one park
29 August 1381	Chigwell	Chikewell	Enclose and impark garden and 50 acres of land within Waltham Forest adjoining manor
4 June 1293	Copped Hall	leCoppedhalle	Enlarge park by 15 acres
12 February 1282	Danbury	Daningbiry	Impark 17 acres wood and 7 acres arable
29 April 1283	Danbury	Daningebory	Impark 10 acres land adjoining park for enlargement of park
28 Aril 1286	Danbury	Danyngebry	Impark grove of 5 acres for enlargement of park
4 June 1280	Gibcrack	Gibbecrak	Enlarge park
5 December 1278	Hallingbury	Cornigehal	Impark wood to enlarge park of Hallingbury
16 January 1336	Halstead	Halstede	Impark wood
25 October 1299	Hanningfield	Hanygfeld	Enlargement by enclosing 11 acres within the forest
1 August 1380	Haroldspark & Copped Hall	Harroldspark & coppedhale park	Licence to enclose 162 acres of demesne lands and a 'perilous lane' to enlarge the park
18 March 1300	Haselden (loc. unknown)	Haseldon	Impark wood
7 June 1280	Horsfrith	Horsfrith	Impark woods
22 October 1336	Ingrave & Great Thorndon	Ingerauf & Great Thorndon	Impark 400 acres meadow pasture and wood
20 October 1264	Layer de Hatley (Layer Marney)	Lyre	Impark wood with hedge and ditch
18 December 1336	Layer de Hatley (Layer Marney)	Leyre	Renewal of licence of 20 October 48 Henry III (1263/40). To enclose 'anew'.
10 March 1380	Little Leighs	Little Leghes	Enclose 100 acres land and wood and make park thereof
17 December 1263	Little Waltham	Little Waltham	Impark 20 acres with hedge and ditch
15 March 1308	Mountnessing	Gynge Mountenye	Impark wood
5 February 1301	Shenfield	Shenefeld	Impark wood
12 December 1264	Stapleford Tawney	Stapleford Taney	Impark wood and 5 acres demesne with hedge and dyke
6 July 1373	Thundersley	Thundresle	Grant in lieu of tithes on land recently included within the park during enlargement
23 May 1247	Tolleshunt	Shyricheshull/Tholeshunt	Licence to re-impark wood
28 April 1286	Waltham (le Pleso)	la Pleso (in Waltham & Hancestre)	Licence to enlarge by enclosing 150 acres of demesne
21 August 1372	White Hall, Dunton	Whitehalle	Impark 300 acres of land
16 January 1377	Wickham	Wykeham	Impark 300 acres adjoining his manor
18 September 1291	Wickney/Wickham (location unknown)	Wykhey	Impark 80 acres
I June 1324	Woolston Hall, Chigwell?	Wolfhampton	Impark 50 acres of land and brushwood

Table 5: List of Grants to Impark contained within the Calendar of Charter Rolls 1227-1516

Date	Modern name	Ancient Name	Comments
26 January 1442	Bocking	Bokking	Impark 200 acres land
15 July 1283	Boreham	Borham	Impark wood with all tillages and lawns adjoining
12 October 1466	Gidea Hall	Gydihall by Romford	Impark 140 acres land, 20 acres wood, 20 acres meadow, 20 acres pasture
12 April 1232	Kelvedon	Kelwedon	Impark wood
1 October 1260	Laindon (Low Leyton?)	Leyndon	Impark 78 acres of wood
14 May 1253	Leyton	Leyton	Impark grove
25 February 1228	Purleigh	Purle	Enclose and impark wood
10 March 1332	Waltham	Waltham	Confirmation of grant of 37 Henry III (1252/3)
24 March 1227	Waltham	Waltham & Harolds Park	Enlargement and grant of fresh imparkment
24 July 1260	Weald	Walde	Impark Wood (poss North Weald Basset or South Weald?)
21 July 1414	West Horndon	West Thorndon	Impark 300 acres land and wood, crenelate lodge in park
5 August 1235	Woodham Ferrers	Wodeham	Cultivate, assart or impark wood

Notes:
Identification of parish/park can be problematical where various spelling/names are used: In addition several entries indexed as 'Essex' in the Calendar of Patent Rolls are not in fact in Essex, these have been omitted where realised. It is possible that there are other Essex entries which have been overlooked due to being mis-ascribed by the indexers to other counties.

Fine Rich Conies or Pernicious Beasts : Rabbits in the Landscape

Michael Leach

2 Landview Gardens, Ongar, Essex CM5 9EQ

'The conies are but a feeble folk, yet make they their houses in the rocks'
(Proverbs 30:26 in the King James Bible of 1611)

Introduction

In the centuries that followed their introduction to England after the Norman Conquest, rabbits were highly prized both for their meat and their fur. As they were poorly adapted to the English climate, their successful breeding required the construction of special enclosures, or warrens, in which they could be contained, fed, protected from predators, and easily harvested when required. In common with other means of production, warrens were often conspicuous features in the medieval designed landscape. This article looks at the growth and decline of rabbit husbandry, and its effect on the landscape of Essex, using both archive and the sparse archaeological evidence from the medieval and early modern periods. Later developments such as hutch breeding, commercial warrens, and the rabbits' adaptation to become a pest, are also examined in the county context. It is hoped that the article will stimulate a greater interest in the vestigial evidence of rabbit warrens in the Essex landscape.

Early History

Though there is some evidence that the Romans may have introduced Mediterranean rabbits to England, they did not survive to naturalise in our relatively hostile climate. There is general agreement that the ancestors of present-day rabbits (usually called coneys in the medieval and early modern periods) were imported, probably from Spain, after the Norman Conquest. They were highly esteemed for their meat (especially in winter when salt meat was the standard fare), and were on the menu before 1220 at Rayleigh in Essex where their bones have been found in the castle midden.[1] The Calendar of Liberate Rolls show that, by the 1240s, large numbers were being supplied by various bishoprics for the king's Christmas celebrations. Rabbits were also highly valued for their fur, particularly the black and the silver, both of which occurred naturally in the wild[2] and well into the nineteenth century, grey rabbit fur was much in demand from hatters. By this time, some country houses (Boyles Court in Brentwood, for example) kept white rabbits as decorative additions to the parkland.[3] Rabbits were also an important source of meat and considerable quantities passed through the London markets from the extensive commercial warrens of the Norfolk Brecklands and elsewhere.

Warrens and Pillow Mounds

Rabbits are now regarded as a serious pest, and it is easy to forget that, when first introduced, they were very ill-adapted to the cold wet British climate. For several hundred years they required careful protection in enclosed warrens, often with the provision of artificial burrows and additional food in winter. Early warrens were often on islands, presumably for reasons of security. The earliest recorded reference to an Essex warren is in 1241, when the bishop of London's warrens at Clacton and Horsey Island supplied 80 live rabbits to a warren in Cheshunt, Hertfordshire.[4] Such warrens were usually enclosed by various combinations of walls, fences, hedges or ditches, in order to keep the rabbits in, as well as to exclude predators and poachers. O. G. S. Crawford, as archaeologist to the Ordnance Survey, was the first to recognise artificially constructed mounds which he termed 'pillow mounds'. These are usually narrow linear banks, often arranged in groups inside some form of protective enclosure, and usually surrounded by a shallow ditch to improve drainage, as rabbits do not thrive in waterlogged burrows. Some were built with internal voids to act as artificial burrows, others had holes bored into them after construction. Housing rabbits in this way probably made it easier to harvest them, as they could be driven out by ferrets and caught in nets pegged over the burrows. It is extremely difficult to date pillow mounds as the burrowing habits of their residents confuse the archaeological stratification; the aptly named Hazeldine Warren, who excavated the High Beech mounds in Epping Forest in the 1925, found a modern high heeled shoe in an archaeological context.[5] The general view is that many of the mounds are post-medieval.[6] However their origins may be more ancient. An illustration in the Luttrell Psalter (c.1325-1335) appears to show black, grey and silver rabbits living in a raised mound and another, in Queen Mary's Psalter of the early fourteenth century, depicts a woman with a ferret on one side of a mound, with an assistant holding a net over a burrow on the other side.[7]

Sometimes older structures, such as long barrows, were adapted to make warrens. A survey of Pleshey castle, Essex, in 1558 indicated that the castle motte was 'nowe replenished wth coneyes', a perfect ready-made warren with good drainage, and already provided with a

Figure 1 The Lady Rabbit Catchers (Royal MS 2 B VII: Queen Mary's Psalter f.155v, early C14 © The British Library Board. All Rights Reserved)

surrounding moat.[8] In other cases the ditches and banks of prehistoric earthworks were adapted to form the enclosure within which new pillow mounds were constructed. There is an Essex example at Little Baddow where pillow mounds (later mistaken for prehistoric barrows) were made within an ancient double bank and ditch.[9] Though it was not unusual for ancient earthworks to be adapted as warrens, occasionally the tables were turned and a warren was turned to advantage in order to defend a military position. During the Civil War, a royalist force took its stand at the top of a hill near Gainsborough, and the warren on its slopes presented a significant obstacle to the attacking parliamentary cavalry. Rabbit warrens, and the problems that they caused to cavalry, were of significance in at least two other Civil War engagements.[10]

In other parts of the country, there is archaeological evidence of pit traps which were constructed in stone on the edge of warren enclosures, both for catching predators and for harvesting the cultivated rabbits. There is no surviving physical evidence of such traps in stone-free Essex, but in 1748 a Swedish visitor to the county described a trap in an unidentified Essex warren. This was made from four planks with a vertical sliding door at each end, activated by a trigger inside the trap. It is interesting to note that this warren was also equipped with traps to capture rabbits attempting to come *into* the warren from the surrounding arable farmland.[11] Clearly all such wooden traps in Essex will have decayed without trace.

Prestige to Pest

It is not clear when rabbits successfully adapted to living in the wild without human assistance and began to become a menace, but it would have been a gradual process. Law makers regarded rabbits as game (i.e. wild animals for hunting) from an early period, as an act of 13 Richard II (1389-90) stated that:

> 'None having land to the yearly value of £10, nor any priest or clerk not in receipt of £10 yearly, should keep greyhound, hound or hunting dog, nor himself use ferrets, heys, nets, harepipes or cords or any other engines to catch deer, hares, rabbits or any other gentleman's game...'

This act is periodically quoted in Essex indictments. In 1591, for example, a man in Shalford was arraigned for the unlawful keeping of 'certaine hayes and engines for the destroyeinge of gentlemen's game'.[12] There is certainly evidence from the seventeenth century that rabbits

Figure 2: In the 16th century black rabbits were valuable for the colour of their coats. (Add. MS 42130: Lutrell Psalter, f.176r, c.1325-35 © The British Library Board. All Rights Reserved.)

were becoming a nuisance. The Essex-born writer, Thomas Tusser, (1523-1580) identified them as a problem for those growing trees from seed:

Sow acorns, ye owners that timber do love,
Sow haw and rye with them, the better to prove,
If cattle or coney may enter to crop
Young oak is in danger, of losing his top.[13]

Another Essex writer, Rev. William Harrison (1534-1593) from Radwinter includes coneys in his chapter entitled 'Of Savage Beasts and Vermins' and categorised them as 'pernicious beasts'.[14] He disapproved of the large number of warrens and wrote

'As for warrens of conies, I judge them almost innumerable and daily like to increase, by reason of the black skins of those beasts are thought to countervail (i.e. exceed) the prices of their naked carcasses, and this is the only cause why the gray are less esteemed'.[15]

Essex Quarter Session indictments hint at this nuisance by showing that rabbits were at large amongst growing crops by the sixteenth century. In 1567, a poacher was accused of breaking into a close at Shenfield and chasing rabbits with greyhounds 'and despoiling [the] growing crops there'.[16] Another particularly detailed indictment of 1600 described how, after dancing at a wedding feast till midnight, two men laid out their net in a wheatfield at South Ockendon 'till the moon was down', and then pitched it on Ockendon Green where they caught one black and one grey coney.[17]

Doubtless the distinction between wild and cultivated rabbits became increasingly blurred. Commons presented another problem, as not only did the wild game belong to the lord of the manor, but also his rabbits were entitled to graze there without infringing the commoners' rights.[18] The lord was also entitled to establish his own warren on common land. In 1613 there was a case in Chancery relating to the Essex manor of Aldersbrook and the rights of the various commoners to establish warrens there.[19] Commoners did not necessarily surrender their grazing rights without a fight; in the 1640s those at Hatfield Forest in Essex repeatedly presented Lord Morley at the manorial court for keeping rabbits and 'for lately making a Warren in the Forest'.[20]

Lords of the manor could also connect their own warrens to the surrounding countryside by openings called 'muses' (sometimes spelt 'meuses'). These allowed the rabbits to roam over a wider area – presumably they ventured out during the day to graze the wastes and common land, returning to the safety of their warren at night. The examination of Robert Fuller in 1580 confirmed that two of his servants had been sent to kill coneys '...... with dogs, jebots and snares in stopping the muses in the pale to the great hurt of the warren' at Stebbing.[21] This suggests that the malefactors closed off the muses so that they could snare the rabbits trying to return to the warren. There are no other Essex documentary references to muses, but whether this indicates that they were rare in the county, or simply not usually of relevance in indictments, is not clear. A jebot was a

raucous sound made on a horn, presumably to panic the rabbits and to make them rush back to the safety of their warren. One would have thought that this practice ran the risk of alerting the owner or warrener to the presence of poachers!

Poachers and Poaching

The indictments of rabbit poachers in Essex provide much information about their activities, as well as a little about the general organisation of warrens. Poachers, like the lawful owners of the warren, mainly used dogs, ferrets and nets to catch the animals. The nets were of two types – purse nets placed over the burrow openings to catch rabbits fleeing from ferrets, and a much longer net called a haye, fixed by pegs or stakes, into which the rabbits were driven by dogs. One Essex haye was described as being '4 to 5 faddomes' in length i.e. about 30 feet long.[22] Another Essex haye in 1606 was said to have been an astonishing 50 fathoms in length i.e. 300 feet. The same indictment refers to 'snares, gins and cords called harepipes'.[23] The harepipe is mentioned in other Essex Quarter Session records (as well as in parliamentary legislation) and was a more robust trap, suitable for catching the larger animal. It is a reminder that some of the mediaeval warrens (the lady's warren at Writtle, for example) did cultivate these animals.[24] Simple wire snares were also used – Sir Thomas Darcy's park keeper at Great Braxted was alerted to poaching when he heard 'two conies squeak' and found the animals caught in this way.[25]

Poachers did not exclusively rely on ferrets, nets and traps. Not infrequently they were armed with swords, fowling pieces, cross bows and staves. These weapons had the additional advantage of providing some protection to poachers when surprised by landowners or warreners, who periodically received a severe beating at the hands of the intruders. There were occasional fatalities amongst the poachers themselves when a gun was discharged accidentally[26] or someone was run through with a sword in the dark.[27] Much of the poaching did take place at night (this is often specified in the indictments) and there were instances where this activity must have been highly organised. In 1598 a resident of Tolleshunt Darcy complained that Edward Tunbridge 'hath for more than twentie yeares continually abused me and others, ... in steelinge my connies, robbing my fishe pondes, taking my paterges and pheasants....'. He also claimed that Tunbridge recruited his helpers from as far afield as 'Baddowe, Danbury, Springfield and other townes in these partes' to raid his and his neighbour's warrens.[28] Sometimes the poaching was on a spectacular scale. In 1563 four men took 16 dozen coneys from a close at Southchurch Hall in a single day in January. Later in the same year, they took 18 dozen from another Southchurch landowner and, the following day, another 15 dozen from Southchurch Hall. There must have been well organised arrangements for carting away and marketing such a large number of rabbits, together with the other game that they were alleged to have taken.[29] This also shows that some warrens contained a substantial number of animals.

Essex Warrens

Unfortunately the identification of specific sites of rabbit warrens in Essex is fraught with difficulties. Though today the name 'warren' is exclusively associated with rabbits, throughout the medieval period it merely indicated a piece of land that was enclosed and preserved for the breeding of game. Thus two men from Good Easter were amerced in the 1430s for taking partridges, pheasants and other birds from the lady's warren at Writtle.[30] Further confusion arises from the term 'free warren'. This did not indicate cultivation of rabbits or an enclosure for breeding, but merely the area over which the lord had the right to hunt for any wild game. Entering and taking a rabbit from the 'free warren' was therefore an offence which could (and frequently did) result in an offender being taken to court. These animals were clearly outside the confines of an enclosed warren, so presumably were wild or at least escapees from captivity. Further difficulties arise from the wording of indictments which frequently refer to breaking into someone's 'close' and taking rabbits. Does this indicate an enclosed warren, or merely trespass on private land for the purpose of catching wild rabbits? However the frequent use of various forms of 'warren', 'coney' and 'clapper' in Essex place-names must indicate that keeping rabbits was very widespread in the county in the past.

Estate maps and Quarter Session records of the sixteenth and seventeenth century also suggest that warrens kept for rearing rabbits were common. Unfortunately evidence for the actual construction and practical management of these warrens is very scanty. Indictments occasionally mention how they were enclosed. In 1607, a close called Clapper Field, part of the manor of Stifford, was 'enclosed by hedges and ditches for keeping, breeding and cherishing coneys'[31] and in 1606, at Hatfield Peverel Priory, 'the close called the Park containing by estimation 7 acres, being enclosed with ditches and fences'.[32] In 1748 Pehr Kalm described an unidentified Essex warren as 'fenced around with planks'.[33] A survey of 1591 mentioned the 'great warren' at Moulsham Hall in Chelmsford, and the Walker estate map of this estate, dated 1593, shows a square enclosure of 7 acres at some distance from the house.[34] Sometimes the description suggests that the arrangement was more informal, with no specific enclosure. In 1616 a Colchester weaver broke into 'various fields at Boxted kept for breeding and nourishing of rabbits'.[35] Possible documentary evidence (albeit somewhat ambiguous) for pillow mounds is found in 1570 when two men were accused of 'breaking into the close called the hills about (the) house (of William Thornton of Woodham Ferris), and taking rabbits with ferrets, dogs, hayes and pursenets'.[36] Late sixteenth and early seventeenth century estate maps provide a little additional evidence. Sometimes the rabbits are shown at large in the park in the company of deer. Other maps of the period indicate pictorially the presence of rabbits within an enclosure, often named 'warren', 'coneyground' and 'coney burrow', but none show any marks suggesting pillow mounds or other structures. Like orchards and hop grounds, they are usually close to the manor or farm house, probably for convenience or to discourage poachers. There is nothing else to suggest that they formed part of a designed landscape, and they do vary considerably in size, shape and position, usually covering from two to seven acres. The estate map of Tolleshunt Darcy in 1692 shows a field called Clapper Hills, perhaps indicating the earlier presence of pillow mounds,[37] but generally estate plans provide disappointingly little evidence about the organisation of warrens, or the significance of their position. There is a clue to the possible site of the former warren of Bicknacre priory in the 1693 survey of Woodham Ferrers. A field near the priory is described as:

> 'The Field now upon Bicknaker Common now or lately belonging to the Priory Farme and was for som time A Warren & now separated from the Common called the Hooe by a ditch in place of the Old Green Bank'.

The 'Old Green Bank' was almost certainly the precinct boundary of Bicknacre priory.[38]

A few groups of pillow mounds have survived in Essex. There are several groups in Epping Forest which, being very poor agricultural land, is exactly where one would expect to find warrens. The solitary one at Little Baddow, built within an earlier earthwork at an unknown date, has already been mentioned. The most impressive survival is the warren in Hatfield Forest, and is probably the one built by Lord Morley in the 1630s to the great annoyance of the commoners. This too was constructed within an earlier ditch and bank enclosure, with about a dozen pillow mounds of various sizes formed on the inner face of the bank, and several free-standing ones in the centre. It is still a rather water-logged site, not particularly suitable for rabbits, though each pillow mound was surrounded by a drainage ditch. The warrener's lodge straddled the bank at one end of the enclosure. In the late 1680s the new owner re-stocked the warren and employed another warrener but, half a century later, it had been abandoned.[39] It is likely that most pillow mounds will have been lost to landscape improvements, or the levelling effect of arable cultivation.

It is surprising to find that pillow mounds were still being constructed as late as the end of the nineteenth century. In 1893 John Simpson, a Yorkshire landowner, advised that 'conical mounds should be thrown up in parallel lines about 100 yards apart. They are easily made and will cost about 9d per cubic yard. They may be about 4 yards wide, and three feet above the ground at the apex'.[40] In Essex, some of the High Beech pillow mounds were made within the living memory of reliable witnesses interviewed by Hazeldine Warren in 1927.[41] It may seem surprising to find that a rabbit warren was regarded as an asset on a country estate at the end of the nineteenth century, but it is probable that it was intended for shooting by the owners and their visitors, and would have been enclosed with a wire netting fence. An example was Hedingham Castle, sold by auction on 13 August 1896. The catalogue noted 'a beautifully undulating park studded with well grown trees and plantations, and includes a rabbit warren and rookery'.[42] Rooks were also shot for sport.

It is disappointing that the poor survival of the physical evidence of warrens in Essex appears to have removed any evidence of their deliberate placement, as well as their religious symbolism, in the landscape. It has been suggested that the large 17 acre rabbit warren at the Castle Hedingham priory, Essex (founded by Aubrey de Vere, first earl of Oxford and owner of the castle) was in a significantly prominent and conspicuous position, intentionally placed adjacent to a religious foundation and clearly visible from the approach road from the south west.[43] Sites elsewhere, such as the Triangular Lodge at Rushton, Northants, indicate that their position could be highly significant, and that the Christian symbolism attached to the rabbit would have been generally understood and easily 'read' in this landscape.[44] At Godolphin House in Cornwall, four pillow mounds were positioned on the brow of a hill where they would have been clearly visible from the house itself.[45] As so little is known about the positioning of warrens in designed Essex landscapes, the appendix to this article is an attempt to identify sites within the county where the vestigial remains of rabbit cultivation might be discovered. Not all of the aggrieved owners whose names appear in the Quarter Session Rolls can be identified and, even where a particular manor is indicated, it is not usually possible to know if the warren was sited close to the house, or elsewhere in the parish. The list is mainly compiled from Quarter Session records, leases and estate maps.

Post-Sixteenth Century

It appears that, by the latter part of the sixteenth century, rabbits had become domesticated. The earliest published work to demonstrate this was that of Robert Payne in 1589, entitled *Directions for keeping Tame Conies*.[46] Hutch-reared rabbits were regarded as more valuable, as they had more meat on them as well as better skins. Gervaise Markham said this about 'boxes for tame conies':

'…one of these fine rich conies…from Martelmas to Candlemas, is worth any fine other conies, for they are of body much fatter and larger and when another skin is worth but 2 pence, they are worth 2 shillings, and are ever at hand for dish without charge of nets, ferrits, or other engines; and give their bodies gratis, for their skinnes will pay their masters charge into a large interest.'[47]

A tame rabbit was noted when the mayor of Colchester entertained the Rev. Ralph Josselin in October 1646. The diarist observed:

'…a tame gelt rabbit, like a little lambe. It weighd about 7[lib] the fatt on the kidney about a pound;'[48]

The indictments give no clues about hutch-reared rabbits in Essex (perhaps because they were too difficult to poach) apart from one reference in 1600 to '…the warren and severall cunny yards of John Hurlestone esq' at Orsett. 'Cunny yards' might suggest enclosed areas where hutches were kept.[49] The impression that hutch rearing became prevalent in the eighteenth century is reinforced by the unknown author of *The Complete Grazier*, published in 1767. Judging from his frequent Essex references, he must have been familiar with the county and the purpose of his book was to help gentlemen to maximise their profits from bees, domestic fowl and rabbits, as well as from cattle, sheep and pigs. The section on rabbits pointedly notes that 'they bring considerably more profit in hutches than in pits' and goes into some detail about the economics of this form of rabbit keeping, noting in addition the benefits of rabbit droppings as fertiliser, and the use of their entrails (after slaughter) for feeding fish in the fish ponds.[50] Collecting rabbit droppings from hutches would have been much easier than from an open warren and, in the mid eighteenth century, these were reckoned to be 'of so hot and fertile a nature to both ploughed and sward ground that it is sold with us for six pence the single bushel trodden in …'[51] By the early nineteenth century, William Cobbett was recommending the keeping of rabbits in hutches by cottagers, both to provide inexpensive meat, as well as to encourage children's interest in animal husbandry. He advised that does should not be permitted more than seven litters a year, or allowed to keep more than six young ones at a time, and gave specific instructions on a suitable diet.[52]

From the evidence of Essex indictments and estate maps, it would appear that the rabbit warrens associated with manor houses had largely disappeared by the end of the seventeenth century, though it is not clear whether this was due to the spread of feral rabbits, the adoption of rearing rabbits in hutches, or rabbit meat falling out of favour for the gentleman's table. The numerous references in the diary of Rev. James Woodforde (1740-1803) would suggest that this Norfolk clergyman, and his gentry friends, were still consuming them in considerable numbers.[53] The decline of domestic warrens coincided with the rise of the large commercial warrens, leased to tenant warreners, often sited on marginal agricultural land. However conflicts arose when these warrens shared land with other tenants who had grazing rights for cattle and sheep, and the proliferation of rabbits led to over-grazing.[54]

It appears that, by the eighteenth century, the only warrens persisting in Essex were commercial ones, probably supplying the London market. For example, in 1779, a 37 acre warren at Goldsmith's Farm on the borders of Romford and Dagenham was leased for an indefinite period at annual rent of £80 and 50 couple of rabbits.[55] However commercial warrens in Essex seem to have been relatively small and never rivalled the size and extent of those in the heathlands of Norfolk Brecklands, or Lakenheath in Suffolk.[56] The Board of Agriculture reports in the early nineteenth century do not list any commercial warrens in Essex.[57] At the turn of the twentieth century, the contributors to the Essex *Victoria County History*, who were very assiduous at recording obscure aspects of the county's rural economy, made no mention of the cultivation of rabbits,[58] though the High Beech warren would have been constructing pillow mounds within living memory. It would seem that Essex never had large commercial warrens on the scale of the East Anglian ones, and only a few small ones (such as the one at High Beech) were still being leased into the nineteenth century. By this date, the county's mixed farming, numerous hedgerows and woodland margins would have provided an ideal habitat for the pro-liferation of wild rabbits, and ensured a plentiful supply for local consumption.

Conclusion

The present day low status of the rabbit makes it easy to forget that it was once an important part of the agricultural economy, as well as an animal of religious symbolic significance. Though virtually no evidence has been found in Essex for the significance of warrens in landscape design, evidence from other counties suggests that owners would have not overlooked their potential, along with other means of production such as dovecotes and fishponds. It is hoped that this article will help to sharpen the curiosity of archaeologists and garden historians when examining the sites of historic parks and gardens, and perhaps help to make sense of otherwise inexplicable findings.

Bibliography

Anon, 1767 *The Complete Grazier or Gentleman and Farmer's Directory*, London

Anon, 1770 *A New and Complete History of Essex by a Gentleman*, Chelmsford

Beresford, J. (ed), 1935 *Woodforde: Passages from…the Diary of a Country Parson*, OUP

Berridge, J, 1923 'Earthworks at Little Baddow' *EAT, ns, 16*

Buchan, J., 1941 *Oliver Cromwell*, The Reprint Society Ltd

Clapham, A.W., 1919 'Pleshey Castle in 1558-9' *EAT, ns, 15*

Cobbett, W., 1822 *Cottage Economy*, (1979 edition, OUP)

Creighton, O.H., 2009 *Designs upon the Land – Elite Landscapes of the Middle Ages*, Boydell

Ellis, W., 1772 *Ellis's Husbandry Abridged & Methodised*, London

Emmison, F. G., 1970 *Elizabethan Life and Disorder*, Essex County Council

Harrison, W., 1587 *The Description of England,* (1994 edition, Washington DC)

Harting, J. E., 1898 *The Rabbit*, Longmans Green

Hinton, M.A.C., 1912 'Vertebrate Remains from the Middens of Rayleigh Castle' *EAT, ns, 12*

Laver, H., 1898 *The Mammals, Fishes and Reptiles of Essex*, Simpkin, Marshall & Co

Lucas, J. (tr.), 1892 *Kalm's Account of his Visit to England on his Way to America in 1748*, (translated from the original published in Stockholm, 1753), London

MacFarlane, A. (ed), 1991 *The Diary of Ralph Josselin 1616-1683*, OUP

Marshall, Mr., 1818 *Review & Abstract of County reports to the Board of Agriculture*, Longman

Page, W., & Round J. H. (eds), 1907 *Victoria County History of Essex*, 2, OUP

Rackham, O., 1993a *The History of the Countryside*, Dent

Rackham, O., 1993b *The Last Forest*, Dent

Sheail, J., 1971 *Rabbits and their History*, David & Charles

Simpson, J., 1893 *The wild rabbit; or rabbit warrens that pay*, Blackwood

Stocker D. & S., 1996 'Sacred Profanity: the theology of rabbit breeding and the symbolic landscape of the warren' in *World Archaeology*, 28, ii

Thirsk, J. (ed), 1985 *Agrarian History of England & Wales*, 5, ii, CUP

Tittensor, A.M. & R.M., 1986 *The Rabbit Warren near West Dean near Chichester*, Ruth & Andrew Tittensor Consultancy

Tusser, T., 1573 *Five Hundred Points of Good Husbandry,* (*Country Life* reprint 1931, London)

Warren, H., 1927 'Excavations in pillow mounds at High Beech' in *Essex Naturalist*, 21

Wells, F., 2004 'The Little Parks of Essex 1100-1600' unpublished UEA PhD thesis

Williamson, T., 2007 *Rabbits, Warrens and Archaeology*, Tempus

References

1   Hinton 1912, 184
2   Sheail 1971, 17
3   ibid, 61
4   CLR 1240-5, 89
5   Warren 1927, 214-226
6   Williamson 2007, 47-53
7   BL Add MS 42130 & Royal MS 2.B.VII f.155v
8   Clapham, 1919, 160
9   Essex HER no:5720; Berridge 1923, 301-3
10 Buchan 1941, 140
11 Lucas 1892, 158-9
12 ERO Q/SR 119/28
13 Tusser 1931, 102
14 Harrison 1589, 326
15 ibid, 254
16 ERO Q/SR 21/32
17 ERO Q/SR 151/86-8
18 Rackham 1993a, 292
19 ERO D/DQs/17
20 Rackham 1993b, 102
21 ERO: Q/SR 77/31,32
22 ERO: Q/SR 169/78
23 ERO T/A 418/208/12
24 ERO D/DP/M192
25 ERO Q/SR 453/59

26 ERO T/A 180/14

27 ERO T/A 418/81/3

28 ERO Q/SR 143/23

29 ERO Q/SR 16/21a

30 ERO D/DP/M236

31 ERO T/A 418/73/3

32 ERO Q/SR 178/89

33 Lucas 1892, 158

34 Anon 1770, 83; ERO D/DP 1/53

35 ERO Q/SBa 1/23

36 ERO Q/SR 32/1

37 ERO D/DHt P1

38 ERO D/DRa/268

39 Rackham 1993b, 162

40 Harting 1898, 41

41 Warren 1927, 224

42 ERO sales catalogue B100

43 Wells 2004, section 7.2

44 Stocker 1996, 265-72

45 Creighton 2009, 114

46 Thirsk 1985, 544

47 Quoted, without the source, in footnote p.123 in 1931 *Country Life* reprint of Tusser's 500 *Points of Good Husbandry*

48 MacFarlane 1991, 71

49 ERO Q/SR 151/38-41

50 Anon 1767, 215

51 Ellis 1772, 104

52 Cobbett 1822, 139 (in 1979 OUP reprint)

53 Beresford 1935, numerous entries indexed under 'Food'

54 Tittensor 1986, 13-22

55 ERO D/DMy/15M50/494

56 Rackham 1993a, 292

57 Marshall 1818

58 Page & Round 1907

Appendix

This appendix lists, by parish, probable and possible warren sites identified from printed and archive sources at the Essex Record Office. The term 'warren' was used broadly for any enclosure for game, rather than one specifically intended for rabbits. However the sources relating to the sites shown below strongly suggest that rabbits were kept. In some instances, for example, the source refers to an 'enclosure for the keeping and breeding of rabbits', and sites described in this way have been noted here as warrens. There are frequent references to 'breaking into the close of … and taking coneys' and it is not usually clear if this refers to a warren, or simply to private land. For completeness, these cases are included in this appendix with the owner's name, but not described as warrens, as the rabbits may have been escapees or wild. Where found in the archive, the name of the landowner, manor or house is included, as well as the name of the warrener (though this was rarely noted). Finally the year and type of document source at ERO is given (A = Assizes; CC = Court of Chancery; CDGL = conveyance, deed, grant or lease; CLR = Calendar of Liberate Rolls; E = estate map or plan; EAT = Transactions of Essex Archaeological Society; I = inquest; MC = manor court roll; Q = Quarter Session rolls; RP= register of Papist estates; S = sales catalogue; VCH = Essex Victoria County History. Printed sources are referenced)

It is inevitable that this search has only revealed a tiny proportion of all Essex warrens. For example, many more (albeit without confirmatory details) can be found in the database of the Essex Place-names Project under variants of the names 'coney', 'burrow' and 'clapper' (www.essex.ac.uk/history/esah/essexplacenames)

AVELEY

Richard Barrett, owner. Rabbit warren. 1695 Q

BARKING

William Nutbrowne, owner. Rabbit warren "the connyver". 1591 Q

BOXTED

?owner. Field for keeping rabbits. ?warren. 1616 ERO Q/Sba 1/23

CASTLE HEDINGHAM

? owner. Rabbit warren in the park. 1896 S

17 acre warren adjacent to priory. Medieval. Unpublished thesis.

CHELMSFORD

Moulsham Hall. Warren of 7 acres. 1591 E

Moulsham Hall. Great warren. 1593 survey in Gentleman's History of Essex

---

CHIGWELL

Sir Robt Adby, owner. Rabbit warren. 1665 Q

CHIPPING ONGAR

James Morrice, owner. Rabbits in Bushie Lease close. 1570 Q

CLACTON

Bishop of London's warren. 1241 CLR

COLCHESTER

Sir Thomas Lucas, owner. Rabbit warren. 1606 Q

DAGENHAM

?owner. "Value" rabbit warren. 1696/7 1697 Q

Goldsmiths Farm. Rabbit warren. 1779 CDGL

John Barker, owner. Rabbit warren. 1699 Q

DOWNHAM

Henry Astlowe, owner. Rabbit warren. 1614 & 1616 Q

EAST HORNDON

Sir John Petre. Close on Ingrave common with rabbits. 1582 Q

EPPING

Copt Hall (Sir Hoyle Finch). Rabbit warren. 1611 Q

FINCHINGFIELD

Spains Hall. Enclosure shown with rabbits 5 acres. 1618 E

FOULNESS

Edward Salmon, owner. Rabbit warren. 1609 Q

GREAT BADDOW
John Pashall, owner. Rabbits. 1582 Q
John Paschall. Rabbit warren. 1595 Q
John Paschall, owner. The warren next to the church. 1604
Q/SR 169/78

GREAT BARDFIELD
Sir Martin Lumley, owner. Rabbit warren. 1692 Q
Sir Martin Lumley, owner. "The Old Warren". 1700 Q

GREAT BRAXTED
Sir Benj. Ayloffe, owner. Rabbit warren. 1660 Q
Sir Thomas Darcy, owner. Rabbit warren. 1686 Q

GREAT ILFORD
Thomas Parker of Osgoods. Close ?with rabbits. 1562 Q
Daniel Bond. Close with ? rabbits. 1583 Q
Toby Gage, owner. Rabbit warren. 1656 Q

GREAT WALTHAM
Richard Everard, owner. Rabbit warren "the Couvere".
1612 Q
Lady Judith Clerke, owner. Rabbit warren. 1641 Q

HALSTEAD
Sir Thomas Gardiner's park. Rabbit warren. 1614 Q

HATFIELD (?)PEVEREL
?owner. The Lord's warren (?hares only) 1340-60 CDGL

HATFIELD PEVEREL
The priory. Rabbit warren. 1606 Q

HIGH LAVER
William Masham, owner. Rabbit warren. 1636 Q

HORSEY ISLAND
Bishop of London, owner. Rabbit warren, 1241 CLR

INGATESTONE
Lady Anne Petre. "le warren" with rabbits. 1580 Q
Hall. Rabbit warren. 1587 Q
Hall. Sir John Petre's warren. 1587 Q

LAINDON
James Harrys, owner. Close with rabbits. 1602 Q

LATTON
Latton Hall. Rabbits shown in "cunnygre" of 2 acres. 1616 E
Marks Hall. Rabbits shown in "launde". 1616 E

LITTLE BADDOW
Le Parke. Rabbits. 1607 Q
Manor of Graces. Rabbit warren. 1621 CDGL

LITTLE BURSTEAD
?owner. Rabbit warren on Botney/Botley common. 1605
ERO T/A 316/105

LITTLE CANFIELD
Manor. "Cunuercrofte" of 5 acres. 1590 E
Lord Maynard, owner. Breeding rabbits. 1645 Q

LOUGHTON
Henry Crooke, owner. Rabbit warren. 1650 Q
Warren House. Rabbit warren, 1742 CDGL

MUCKING
?owner. Rabbit warren. 1606 Q

ORSETT
John Hurlestone, owner. Rabbit warren & yards. 1600 Q
Mr Harriston, owner. Rabbit warren. 1600 Q

PLESHEY
Rabbit warren on 'castle hill'. 1558/9 EAT, ns, 15,160
James Keyme, owner. Rabbit warren. 1600 Q
John Keame, owner. Rabbit warren. 1601 Q
Judith Clarke, owner. Lease of warren. 1637 ERO D/DSp
T19 1/12

RAMSDEN BELLHOUSE
Manor. Rabbits shown in park. 1615 E

RAYLEIGH
Mr Bode, owner. Rabbits. 1577 T/A 428/1/41

RETTENDON
See: Wm Thornton at Woodham Ferrers

RIVENHALL
Hall. Park with stock of rabbits. 1700 D/DXr/48

ROMFORD
Manor of Marks. Rabbit warren ('Marks Warren'). 1718 CDGL
Manor of Marks. Rabbit warren. 1760 CDGL

ROYDON
Roydon Hall, warren. 1530. VCH viii, 236

ROXWELL
Newlands Hall. "Greenbury" warren. 1618 CDGL
Newlands Hall. "Greenbury" close 4 acre rabbit warren.
1620 CC

SHEERING
Oxlese warren. 1416. VCH viii, 245.

SHENFIELD
Christopher Harrys, owner. Rabbits. 1567 Q

SOUTH HANNINGFIELD
Margaret Ayloff. "Le warren" with rabbits. 1580 Q

SOUTH OCKENDON
Belhus. The old warren. 1625 CDGL
Manor, William Peter, owner. Rabbit warren. 1641 I

SOUTH WEALD
William Truelove, owner. Rabbit warren. 1689 Q
Thomas Manby of Bawdes. Warren with 70 rabbits. 1730 RP

SOUTHCHURCH
Hall. Rabbits. 1563 Q
Beches. Rabbits. 1563 Q
Robert Lawson, owner. Rabbits. 1563 Q

STANFORD RIVERS
William Wood's close "Brykell Field" with rabbits. 1562 Q

STANWAY
Edward Bockinge, owner. Close with rabbits. 1575 Q
Manor of Olivers. Rabbits in "Coneyborough Field". 1658 E

STAPLEFORD ABBOTS
Albyns. Rabbit warren. 1686 Q

STEBBING
Stebbing Hall/Porters Hall. Warren with rabbits. 1629 EAT
ns xv, 139

STIFFORD
Close of William Latham. "Clapper Field" warren. 1606
T/A 418/73/3
Thomas Wooders, warrener. Stifford rabbit warren. 1645 Q
Warren Farm, site of former warren. 1777. VCH viii, 25
Coney Hall, rabbit warren, 1644/5. VCH viii, 30.

THEYDON GARNON
William Willis, owner. Rabbit warren. 1691 Q

THEYDON MOUNT
William Smythe, owner. Rabbits. 1588 T/A 428/1/74

THURROCK
Edward Keighley.owner. Rabbit warren "Grayes warren".
1618 Q
Edward Keighley, owner. "Grayes Wood" rabbit warren.
1620 Q

TOLLESHUNT DARCY
F. Harve, owner. Rabbit warren. 1598 Q
Mistress Wilson, owner. Rabbit warren. 1598 Q

WANSTEAD
Manor of Aldersbrook. Warren on the common. 1613 CC
Aldersbrook (Mr Lethieullier, owner). Former warren.
1740 E

WENNINGTON
?owner. Aveley marsh warren. 1609 ERO D/DL/T1/705a

WEST BERGHOLT
Waldegrave Abell, owner. Rabbits. 1607 Q
Bergholt Hall. Warren 1516. VCH x, 30

WEST HAM
Capt. Wm Abraham Cooke. Rabbit warren. 1685 Q
Thomas Hawtrell, owner. Rabbit warren. 1693 Q

WEST HORNDON
Lady Petre, owner. Rabbit warren. 1692 Q
Lord Petre, owner. Rabbits. 1663 Q

WEST THURROCK
William Willys, owner. 1597 Q

WETHERSFIELD
Sir John de Neville, owner. Rabbit warren. 1347 & 1355
CDGL
William Deane, owner. Rabbit warren. 1579 Q

WILLINGALE
Manor of Wardens Hall. 9 acre warren & orchard. 1617
CDGL

WITHAM
?owner. Woodgrange rabbit warren. 1666 Q

WIVENHOE
Lord of manor. Warren. 1524 & 1605 MC

WOODHAM FERRERS
Bicknacre Common. Former warren (?of priory) 1693 E
Close called "the hills" about Wm Thornton's house (with
rabbits). 1570 Q

WOODHAM WALTER
Henry Thomas, warrener. Rabbit warren. 1675 A

WRITTLE
The Lady's warren. 1385 CDGL
?owner. Hare and rabbit warren. 1477/8 MC

A Duffus in the Grounds: A Consideration of Some Essex Dovecotes

Mrs Sally-Ann Turner

The Coach House, 49 West Street, Coggeshall, Essex, CO6 1NS

*'... grey-wing'd doves
Around the mossy dovecotes fly.'[1]*

Introduction

This article will briefly examine the historical background of dovecotes in general and focus in detail on some of the surviving examples in Essex. The author's research has concentrated primarily on dovecotes that are now situated within private gardens and the article will therefore also consider how such historic buildings are used in their present setting and how, if at all, they feature in modern garden design. The use of purpose-built dovecotes primarily for the housing of large flocks of pigeons as a source of food started to decline approximately two centuries ago; but many dovecotes have survived throughout the country. Dovecotes tended to be substantially built and investment in such a building probably owed nearly as much to its image as a status symbol as to the provision of fresh meat. Essex has a considerable number of free-standing dovecotes although it has not been possible during the present research to ascertain the exact number of those still extant.

Doves and pigeons are members of the bird family *Columbidae* and both are thought to have descended from *Columba livia*, the blue rock pigeon or dove. The two names are often interchangeable and Roberts & Gale claim that 'Structurally there is no difference between pigeons and doves, but in general, if a pigeon is small, dainty and attractive it is normally referred to as a dove. There are also differences in the shape of the head.'[2] Smith claims that a fundamental difference between the two, with significance for the dovecote owner, is that the pigeon is a gregarious bird liking to live in flocks with a natural homing instinct whereas the dove tends to live in pairs and 'it has never been so thoroughly domesticated as a pigeon ... ; it is a true migrant and assembles in flocks only for migration'[3,4] Thus, it should be remembered that the adult birds inhabiting the dovecote were usually free to come and go and rarely prevented from leaving. Over the centuries the specially constructed buildings used to house the birds have been called various names including columbarium in Roman times; culverhouse (the Anglo-Saxon word for pigeon being 'culver'); pigeon or dovehouse; pigeon or dovecote and, particularly in Essex, duffus.[5] For the purpose of this article the birds will be referred to as pigeons and the buildings as dovecotes.

In the past, various articles on historic dovecotes have estimated that there were 26,000 pigeon-houses in England in the seventeenth century. McCann however questions the accuracy of this statement and provides well-researched information to dispute the claim.[6] Dovecotes tend to be built of vernacular materials and the fact that a good number have survived throughout the country must in part be due to the quality of the workmanship of their builders. It is not known how many have been lost but the 1995 Monuments Protection Programme report by English Heritage assessed the total number of extant dovecotes to be 2059, based on the Sites and Monuments Record and other sources.[7] Most dovecotes are now protected either as listed buildings or scheduled monuments.

Historic Background

Archaeological finds suggest that early man, living and sheltering in caves, ate pigeon meat and as rock doves nested in such caves it is thought that primitive man may have taken young birds from their nests for food. However, the practice of actually keeping pigeons as a source of meat probably originated in the Middle East. An Egyptian painting on the tomb of Sebekhotpe in Thebes, c1420 BC, depicts a pigeon on its house which suggests early evidence of dovecotes.[8] It is thought that the custom may have been introduced to Britain by the Romans although it is not known when dovecotes actually first appeared as none are recorded in the Domesday Book. The earliest known documentary

Figure 1 A pigeon perched on twentieth century louver of an old dovecote.

evidence for dovecotes in England dates from the middle of the twelfth century, and the oldest known *extant* dovecote in the country was built, according to its inscription, in 1326 at Garway in Herefordshire.[9] This was on a Knights Templar site and many other early freestanding dovecotes were associated with religious orders. The two oldest surviving dovecotes in Essex (both listed as Grade II*) date from the fifteenth century or possibly earlier.

The historic legal aspects of both owning a dovecote and the keeping of pigeons are both interesting and rather complex.[10] The right to build and keep a dovecote was a matter of common law and originally the high cost of building and stocking one ensured that only the wealthiest lords could afford it. By the fourteenth century the ownership of a dovecote was regarded as the prerogative of the lord of the manor and even when, for economic reasons, manors were leased it was only the landlord who could build a dovecote should his tenant want one where none had existed before. Some lords, when establishing clergy on their estates, granted the parish priest the right to keep pigeons although it is unlikely that this privilege was extended to manors that had an existing dovecote. During the sixteenth century land formerly owned by religious establishments were sold as intact manors: 'As before the Dissolution dovecotes were still associated with the privileges of lordship. Indeed that was a large part of their appeal, for many of the lawyers, officials and younger sons of land-owning families ... were actively engaged in establishing their new social position. One way of asserting the status as manorial lords was to build a conspicuous dovecote near the manor house.'[11]

Manorial prerogative was undermined following a court judgement in 1619 which determined 'that the erecting of a dove-cote by a freeholder, who is not lord of the manor, nor owner of the rectory, and replenishing it with doves, is not any nuisance inquirable or punishable in a leet.'[12] By the later eighteenth century pigeon-keeping had generally ceased to be seen as a manorial prerogative and dovecotes were commonly erected by non-manorial landowners. Smith quotes from an article in *The Complete Farmer* written in 1766: '... pigeon houses are common on many farms...'[13] and it is assumed that such dovecotes tended to be built within the farmyard either as free-standing units or annexed to other buildings on site.

Pigeons, (rather than doves), were kept in dovecotes in order to provide a regular supply of tender meat in the form of unfledged birds, known as squabs, whose muscles hadn't been toughened by flying. In general pigeons mate for life and a pair of adults is capable of producing two chicks approximately six times a year for about seven years.[14] Each spring it was advisable to spare the first brood of chicks and allow them to grow to maturity and breed that same year. Squabs were thus usually available for the table from April until October, but not throughout the winter as some past writers have suggested. McCann uses convincing documentary evidence to challenge the previously held theory that tender pigeon meat was available throughout the

harshest winter months and this, in turn, negates an oft quoted reason for the decline of dovecotes being the introduction of cheap root crops such as turnips that were used to feed livestock throughout the winter in order to provide a year-round meat supply.[15] McCann maintains: 'The truth is that before the late eighteenth century ... dovecotes were expensive prestige buildings whose only economic function was to provide an additional delicacy for those who already had plenty of other fresh meat...'[16]

An added bonus of pigeon-keeping was the dung that accumulated on the dovecote floor which tended to be lower than the level of the doorway for practical purposes. Winter was considered to be the best time to remove it in order to avoid disturbing the sitting birds during the breeding season. Incidentally, as old birds tended to be culled towards the end of the year, winter was also the best time to clean and repair the dovecote. Thomas Tusser, who was born in Essex c1524, gave advice for each month in *Five Hundred Points of Good Husbandry*, published c1573. For January he wrote:

'Feed Doves, but kill not,
if loose them ye will not.
Dovehouse repaire,
make Dovehole faire.
For hop ground cold,
Dove doong woorth gold.'[17]

Pigeon dung was prized as a valuable fertilizer and Smith mentions that in *Samuel Hartlib, his Legacy, or an Enlargement of the Discourse of Husbandry used in Brabant and Flanders* (published 1659) Hartlib wrote that 'Pigeon's or Hen's Dung is incomparable. One load is worth ten loads of other dung...'[18] The tanning industry used pigeon dung for the softening of leather and in the early seventeenth century it provided an important source of saltpetre for gunpowder manufacture. Together with those from other farm birds, the feathers and down of the pigeons were used for stuffing pillows and mattresses.[19] In addition both pigeons and their dung were used in medicinal remedies in the Middle Ages.[20]

Pigeons required minimal basic care once they had been established in the dovecote. They usually only needed supplementary feed during harsh winter weather and normally spent most days foraging for food in the surrounding area. This foraging was however a contentious issue. It was estimated that a pair of birds could consume four bushels of corn in a year and as pigeons were given manorial protection and allowed to forage freely in large numbers, the crop losses could be significant. This became an especial issue during the Napoleonic Wars (1799-1815) when wheat prices were high and many landowners, farming their own newly-enclosed lands, became aware of the crop losses caused by pigeons. McCann quotes contemporary writers on the subject including St John Priest, writing in 1810 about pigeons in Buckinghamshire: 'The injury done by them on the crops ... more than counterbalances any advantage from their manure, or from themselves as food'.[21] Although peasants had long suffered from their lord's pigeons feeding off their crops, the decline in the use of dovecotes appears to have occurred from 1800s when it was in the economic interests of the landowner to reduce the numbers of pigeons kept. It is thought that those reduced flocks tended to be fed more as farmyard poultry or housed well away from vulnerable crops. This resulted in some dovecotes being demolished, especially in grain-producing areas, or abandoned; some were made into granaries and others were converted into dual purpose buildings by the addition of flooring to create one or two extra storeys, with the pigeons occupying the upper level. Several Essex examples show evidence of such conversions, mostly comprising two-storeyed buildings but at least one, in the Gestingthorpe area, has three storeys. Other reasons given for the decline of the large dovecote from the 1800s included the emergence of larger farms being managed professionally together with transport improvements which meant farm produce, including birds like geese, hens and turkeys, could be delivered more quickly and there was less need for country communities to be so self-sufficient.[22] However some dovecotes were still built during the nineteenth century, for example at Battlesbridge, Essex, where an octagonal, brick dovecote on a site, formerly known as Duffus Farm, bears the inscription 'W.B. 1819'.[23] McCann gives a Yorkshire example of an old isolated dovecote being replaced in 1846 by a new and productive pigeon-tower within the farmyard.[24] However, most nineteenth century dovecotes tend to be two-storey, dual-purpose buildings with pigeons occupying the upper storey and the lower storey being used either for storage or for the housing of other animals, such as horses or poultry.

Siting and Design of Dovecotes

Siting of a dovecote was important both to the owner and the birds: Those owners wishing to flaunt their right to have a dovecote might want it to be in a conspicuous place where its value as a status symbol would be fulfilled. For security reasons however it was wise to have the dovecote relatively close to the house itself, and also to ensure that the dovecote door faced the house or farm buildings where it could be easily observed, usually by servants, as a deterrent against theft. Security became even more of a concern during the nineteenth century when shooting clubs needed large numbers of live birds and whole flocks were stolen. The octagonal brick dovecote at High House, Purfleet, had the added security feature of having an inner metal door presumably as a deterrent against theft. The siting of the dovecote away from trees, where hawks might be lurking, in a position that offered the pigeons a clear view of their surroundings together with being within approximately thirty metres of human activity also helped protect against attack from flying predators. Several of the Essex dovecotes visited were positioned fairly close to the kitchen where security of the birds could be monitored. A good water supply was essential and the author noted that three dovecotes visited were positioned adjacent to a moat and two were near a horse pond. Incidentally pigeons are peculiar in that they drink by taking long draughts whereas most birds tip back their heads in

Figure 2 *A dovecote near Harlow is reflected beautifully in the moat.*

order to swallow.

Pigeons enjoy sitting in a sunny spot sheltered from the wind and the design of many dovecotes incorporates the provision of suitably positioned sloping roofs and ledges. Many dovecotes had pyramidal roofs which offered perching opportunities on the side away from the wind direction that day. The access to the dovecote needed be just large enough for the pigeons to get through whilst restricting access to bigger predatory birds. With many dovecotes such access was at the apex of the roof via a rectangular turret called a louver that usually had slanted boards horizontally fixed about 15cms (six inches) apart to each side, between which the birds could come and go. The roofs of some dovecotes culminated in a square tower with four-gabled openings, which also provided sheltered perching opportunities on all sides; whilst others had vented gablets on the hipped roofs. In addition, some dovecotes, including at least five in Essex, had gabled dormers and their roofs also offered perching places. Generally, windows in dovecotes were kept to a minimum and tended to have protective coverings such as metal grills to keep out birds of prey or, in some cases, they were glazed.

The sixteenth century rectangular dovecote at Tolleshunt D'Arcy Hall has a pair of small arched windows which retain some contemporary wood-fired glass.[25] As their descendants inhabited caves, pigeons should be at home in fairly dark places but the pigeon-keeper would find it useful to have some light from a window in order to see the squabs he needed to collect.

Figure 3 The pipe in a dovecote near Harlow.

Many dovecotes had a pulley-operated trap door attached to the louver in order to confine birds when required and to prevent access at night by predators. Birds of prey are the main predators of pigeons, mainly outside but also inside if they gained access to the dovecote. As a means of preventing such entry, some dovecotes were fitted with an internal structure called a pipe which was usually a wooden frame or chute, smooth on the inside to prevent perching opportunities, which was suspended from the louver. Pigeons could ascend and descend through it easily but sparrow-hawks could not. Pipes are still to be found in at least two Essex dovecotes; one at Olivers in Stanway and the other near Harlow.

Pigeons are most vulnerable when taking off and prefer high perches from where they can swoop down and pick up speed more quickly if hunted. 'Pigeon-keepers of all periods have recognised that it is desirable to build the dovecote high. Often it is sited on the highest ground available; where it is free-standing its most characteristic form is the tower.'[26] Most dovecotes are comparatively tall in relation to their floor plan which, in addition to providing more nesting space, would give the necessary height required. As alternatives to the basic tower design, beehive and lectern shaped dovecotes also existed, most frequently in Scotland.

Human access to the dovecote was through a small, low doorway which tended to be just large enough for a man to block with his body in order to prevent birds escaping. The doorway was also kept as small as possible in order to restrict the size of the silhouette of the person entering so as not to frighten or unsettle the breeding birds more than was necessary. Most doors were of simple wooden construction although some doorways were more ornate than the usual rectangular ones.

Limiting the number of windows and having a small doorway allowed more nest-boxes to be incorporated within the dovecote and a few very large ones had 2500 or more nest-boxes, although the usual number ranged between 300 and 1000. Owing to their breeding cycle, one pair of pigeons would make use of two nest-boxes

with the hen incubating a new clutch of eggs before her last pair of squabs had reached maturity. The largest Essex example is an octagonal, brick dovecote at Wendon Lofts, which Smith records as having 1500 timber nest-boxes.[27] Until the appearance of the carnivorous brown rat (*Rattus norvegicus*), into England in c1729, nest-boxes lined the internal walls of a dovecote from floor to ceiling. After the brown rat became more common advice given in publications such as the *The Sportsman's Directory* of 1735 was for the sides of internal walls to be smooth from floor level to approximately four feet (120cms) in order to minimise attack.[28] The brown rat can gnaw through lath and plaster and many owners responded to this threat by replacing the in-fill of their timber-framed dovecotes with brick walls to a height of four feet. The octagonal timber-framed dovecote at Olivers near Colchester has such a brick plinth as do many other Essex examples.

Nest-boxes were obviously a very distinctive feature of dovecotes and the finding of nest-box remains in or near a derelict or demolished building can be a very helpful means of identifying the site of a former dovecote as was the case at Pigeon Mount near Brentwood.[29] Nest-boxes were often constructed of timber or brick but other materials were used including clay-bat which comprised unfired blocks of clay mixed with straw.[30] Clay-bat nest-boxes were less durable and the fact that some have survived in the dovecote at Olivers in Stanway has resulted in this being designated as a scheduled monument (confirmed in 2000). Nest-boxes in medieval dovecotes were incorporated into the main walls which tended to be very thick. By the eighteenth century dovecote walls tended to be thinner, which meant that

Figure 4 The timber-framed dovecote at Olivers, Stanway, showing the brick plinth.

the nest-boxes were either constructed separately against the walls or partly integrated, as was discovered when the Downham Hall brick dovecote was dismantled and rebuilt near the church.[31]

Early nest-boxes were basic spaces built into the thickness of the dovecote walls; but in time L-shaped ones were used in order to provide extra room for the bird's tail and to give a more enclosed space for the two young squabs. Many dovecotes had alighting ledges, often made of brick or wood, which jutted out from the internal walls and enabled the adult birds to enter and leave the nest-boxes more easily. Arrangements varied and alighting ledges could be provided either at the base of each row of nest-boxes or every second, third or fourth tier or, in some cases, not at all. The Tolleshunt D'Arcy dovecote has well-preserved brick L-shaped nest-boxes with alighting ledges along every second tier.

Some dovecote interiors show evidence of having been painted white as a result of the traditional practice of coating the internal walls with lime-wash. Early writers had suggested that pigeons were attracted to white surfaces, but by the eighteenth century an annual lime-washing of the internal walls was advocated as a precaution against insect infestation.

As squabs were regularly taken from the dovecote, easy access to all the nest-boxes was a practical requirement and in many cases this was accomplished by the use of a revolving ladder which was fixed to a frame radiating from a central post rising from the middle of the floor and secured in the roof. This structure is also known as a potence. The revolving ladder was most useful in circular dovecotes but could also be used in square, octagonal, hexagonal ones. However, it did not provide a suitable means of access to enough nest-boxes in a rectangular dovecote.

Essex Dovecotes

The first stage of the current research was to ascertain the location of extant dovecotes in Essex. *Pigeon Cotes and Dove Houses of Essex*[32] listed fifty-nine dovecotes known to have existed in 1931. Of these, two comprised gable-ended sections within other buildings (Ingatestone and Chignall St James); one was of recent construction (Witham); one had been converted into a cottage (Farnham); one is now in Cambridgeshire (Gt Chishill); five were thought to have been demolished or in a ruinous condition (Birchanger, Gt Bardfield, Gt Maplestead, Steeple Bumpstead and West Thurrock); two could not be traced (Wakes Colne and Widdington) and two are now within new housing developments (Newport and Purfleet). The author wrote to forty-five owners asking for information on the present state of their dovecotes. Twenty-six replies were received, of which three owners reported that their dovecotes were no longer extant; two preferred not to be included in the research; two claimed their buildings to be granaries and one reported that the dovecote had been moved (from Downham Hall and re-sited next to Downham Church). Furthermore Pimp Hall dovecote, which Smith describes as 'possibly the most picturesque in Essex', is now in the London Borough of Waltham Forest. The author is still trying to assess the

Figure 5 Substantial beams in the dovecote near Thaxted which originally may have been a gatehouse.

exact number of extant dovecotes within the modern boundary of Essex but estimates that there is a minimum of 48 of which eleven of them appear to have been converted into two-storey buildings and at least one three-storey conversion survives. The author visited twelve dovecote sites, although some are not mentioned by name at the request of the owners. Interestingly the distribution is concentrated more in the northwest of the county with the majority in the Braintree and Uttlesford districts. Whilst most dovecotes were purpose built, there are two in Essex, both considered to be the oldest surviving dovecotes in the county that were formerly used for other purposes: one is situated in the Thaxted area and is thought to have been a gatehouse originally – the substantial internal beam work would support this.

The other is near Witham within a moated site and is thought to have been built c1400 as a medieval kitchen. Although other detached or partially attached medieval kitchens have been recorded this one is unusual in having been square on plan, each side measuring approximately 6.8 metres, rather than rectangular which was more traditional. When the Hall was relocated during Tudor times the timber-framed building was no longer required for culinary purposes and it was converted into a dovecote. Following an assessment of the building, listed building consent was granted in 1998 for it to be converted into an office.[33]

In 1931 Smith observed:

'As with her churches, Essex is rich, not so much with outstanding examples, though such an example as that at Wendon Lofts would be difficult to beat, but with the variety of building material, and the variety of shape. Building materials range from early Tudor brickwork, weather boarding, lath and plaster, "clay-bat", rubble, flint, and brick noggin, and this variety is not expressed according to district, but occurs in delightful juxtaposition...... Not only the material but the shape is exquisitely varied.' [34]

Present research indicates that the majority of surviving Essex dovecotes are roughly square on plan, are either brick-built or timber-framed and have either a pyramidal roof topped by a louver or a hipped roof with vented gablets at either end. There are various combinations of design elements such as timber-framed dovecotes with brick in-fill and there are at least two with pyramidal roofs topped by four-gabled openings. The smallest square dovecote visited was near Thaxted, which has sides approximately three metres in length whilst the largest one visited, near Dunmow, has sides just over six metres long. No revolving ladder has survived in the Essex sites visited by the author but it is known that one was used in the Grade II* octagonal dovecote at Wendon Lofts (now a scheduled monument), and also in the octagonal ones at Downham near Wickford and High House in Purfleet. Revolving ladders may have existed in other Essex dovecotes but these would have been dismantled when additional floors were added mainly during the nineteenth century when many dovecotes were converted into dual-purpose buildings.

Essex has one surviving circular dovecote which is in the Writtle area. It is located in permanent pasture, which formerly may have been a kitchen garden, approximately thirty metres from the house. The dovecote is two-storey and brick-built with a conical tiled roof topped by a weather-vane, the original louver being no longer present. The only other circular Essex dovecote was at Rochford Hall, thought to date from c1540 and was thatched. Unfortunately in 1888 it was destroyed by fire following lightning damage.[35] Essex also has at least four rectangular and six octagonal dovecotes. The only known Essex dovecote with an irregularly-shaped floor plan was recorded at Earls Colne Priory as comprising three sides of a rectangle with the south side replaced by three sides of a hexagon.[36] This building has not been found in any listed buildings information and is thought to have been lost. Two regular hexagonal dovecotes are known to have existed in the county: The one at Battlesbridge has been mentioned already and the other was on the former Bower Hall estate in Steeple Bumpstead. Sadly it was demolished in 1955 for the sake of its bricks.[37] Smith's description suggests it to have been both functional and attractive in its orchard setting beside a piece of water. Built c1700, it is shown on an oil painting (ERO: 1/Mb 62/1/6 photo of original) which has been attributed to Knyff (1710) showing the extensive estate of Bower Hall. It stood on six corner piers linked by rounded arches. The steep tiled roof was surmounted by a bell-shaped louver, topped by a weather vane. Smith's illustration shows circular windows on two sides and the whole building reflected in the water would have made an impressive focal point.[38]

Dovecotes and the Designed Landscape of Essex Past and Present

This leads us to consider the dovecote in the designed landscape. Early examples were intended to impress, in addition to fulfilling their functional aims, and their placement would have been chosen accordingly. By the eighteenth century, wealthy owners were appreciating

STEEPLE BUMPSTEAD.

Figure 6 An image of the lost dovecote formerly at Bower Hall, Steeple Bumpstead, taken from Donald Smith's The Pigeon Cotes and Dove Houses of Essex, *London: Simpkin Marshall, 1931, p235.*

the decorative potential of dovecotes. Their construction might reflect the architectural style of the period, and possibly be used to enhance the immediate landscape. The eighteenth century is also the period when more polygonal dovecotes, particularly octagonal ones, appear. Hansell suggests:

'It was not until the eighteenth century that their ornamental aspect was exploited, some even being sited in the newly fashionable landscaped gardens of the day. During this period it was common practice to disguise utilitarian buildings of all sorts with an elegant façade and incorporate them as eyecatchers within the grounds ... Many of these later dovecotes were constructed by local builders, sometimes supervised by their patron with pattern book in hand, but there are several still in existence which were designed by well-known contemporary architects.'[39]

During the late 1740s and early 1750s the landscape designer and architect, Sanderson Miller, is thought to have designed the dovecote in the park at Wroxton Abbey in Oxfordshire in addition to several other features.[40] Whilst either William Kent or William Smith of Warwick may have been responsible for designing the classical temple, housing both a dovecote and stable, which was built at Barrington Park in Gloucestershire.

Figure 7 The sixteenth century dovecote at Tolleshunt D'Arcy Hall serves as a focal point in the north-east corner of the moated site. The central louver is a later eighteenth century addition.

This building served as an impressive focal point in the landscaped grounds in addition to its functional use.[41]

An impressive Essex example may have stood in Thorndon Park, near the site of the old Thorndon Hall. The earthwork on which it stood, known as Pigeon Mount, was excavated in 1995 to reveal the foundations of an octagonal structure on the mound along with large quantities of baked clay, thought to represent the remains of nesting boxes, suggesting that a large dovecote stood on the mound in the eighteenth century. Plans from 1733 depict a spiral path ascending to the top of the mound and it is probable, given its position in the centre of the formal gardens, that the mound served as both viewing platform and the base of a dovecote.[42, 43] Another Essex example of an attractive dovecote situated in a former parkland setting is that at Hedingham Castle where the brickwork dates to c1720 although an earlier dovecote was recorded on the site in 1592.[44] This octagonal dovecote, with a glazed lantern instead of a louver, is supported by low brick piers at each corner. It is situated to the southeast of the house and Norman keep, in a sheltered and level position, on a gradient falling steeply towards a lake to the southwest. The surrounding trees and shrubs are of no great age suggesting that originally the dovecote stood as a clearly visible focal point.

In addition to dovecotes being used for ornamental purposes, the birds themselves were considered by some owners to add value to the landscape. Obviously ornamental doves can be very attractive birds whether seen flying over the landscape or perched on a roof and during the eighteenth century a trend developed for gentlemen to keep ornamental breeds for pleasure;[45] but others may have found pleasure in watching the antics of the common pigeon!

If dovecotes were originally considered as part of the designed landscape, how do they fit with the present

landscapes in their immediate vicinity? It was noted that at several of the garden sites visited the dovecote was of a similar age to that of the principal building and built of similar materials. In the author's opinion, this helps to ensure that a dovecote fits comfortably within its setting even if the house has been extended and/or its orientation altered; or if the area surrounding the dovecote has changed over the years from being, for example, in a farmyard setting to becoming part of the modern garden. Whilst the usage and possible adornment of the grounds may have been altered once or several times, the fact that the buildings are contemporary, or appear to be so, brings a certain harmony to the site. A good example of an Essex dovecote sitting very harmoniously within its setting is to be found at Tolleshunt D'Arcy Hall where a single-storey rectangular sixteenth century dovecote, built of the same red brick as the Tudor hall, is situated in a moated site within an old walled garden.

Tolleshunt D'Arcy Hall has a very interesting history and entering the site, across a wonderful Tudor bridge, is like stepping back in time. The kitchen garden has low box hedging lining its straight paths and one's eye is led along one of two paths which lead to the dovecote, sitting very comfortably in the north-east corner. It serves as a very appropriate focal point for that side of the garden whilst the nearby church provides a suitable eye-catcher beyond the wall in the opposite corner. The former first-floor solar of the Hall had a large window which would have provided a good view of the dovecote in past centuries.

Another example of a historically interesting setting is the site near Thaxted where the dovecote and its principal building, a fine example of an old hall house, are both listed as being fifteenth century or earlier. The dovecote is two-storey and timber-framed with original chamfered braces forming the entrance arch on the north-east side and saltyre bracing to the lower wall frames on the north-west side. The walls are part weather-boarded

Figure 8 Fifteenth century dovecote near Thaxted originally built as a gatehouse.

Figure 9 The dovecote at Woolpits, overlooking the site of a former kitchen garden, serves as an attractive focal point from various aspects of the garden.

and part plastered and the hipped roof is red tiled with gablets to south-east and north-west. The dovecote stands to the south-west of the house on the roadside boundary, making it a very appropriate position for a gatehouse, which is what it was thought to have been originally. The entrance to the site is now on the northern side so that the dovecote sits snugly within the garden in the corner of the front lawn and provides a focal point from the principal rooms of the house. It has a flower border to the west and a shrubbery to the east so that it is framed on either side by plants. Small windows either side of twentieth century double doors with semi-circular brick steps in front of them suggest that it may have been used as a summer-house in the past. It is currently used for storage and, as is the case at other sites, the owner fully appreciates its historic value.

The owner of Woolpits in Bardfield Saling regards her dovecote very much as an integral part of its site and explained that during Victorian times her dovecote was used for its intended purpose and was situated adjacent to what had been a large kitchen garden. She expressed appreciation of it in the following way, 'The dovecote, which can be seen from many angles of the garden is a beautiful feature and firmly fixes the whole property in the ingenuity and prosperity of the Victorian era.'[46] The dovecote, which is listed as seventeenth century, now has two storeys and stands approximately fifteen metres from the house. The walls are of brick to a height of approximately 1.70 metres with lath and plaster above. The red-tiled pyramidal roof has a square louver with sides which are now boarded and a weathervane completes the picture. It was carefully renovated in 2008.

On its north side the dovecote overlooks the site of the old kitchen garden which has been grassed over with dwarf box hedges outlining its former position. To the south and east the dovecote is framed by grass whilst at the base of its west side, facing the house, is a flower bed that links the dovecote to the small ornamental paved garden near the house and helps to create a courtyard feel to that secluded area.

Another dovecote that serves to enhance its setting is in the Harlow area and will be referred to as the Harlow dovecote. Figure 11 shows its south-west aspect beautifully positioned by the moat with the exuberant planting of the rose garden edging the water.

To the west, this red brick-built dovecote forms a focal point in the rose garden although it is teasingly partially hidden by trees and shrubs as one enters that sheltered area which was full of the fragrance of roses when visited in June. The rose garden was designed in 1983 and the dovecote was integral to the design. The dovecote is single-storey and thought to have been used earlier in the twentieth century as a stable which would explain the larger size and style of the present door. Mature shrubs and ornamental trees screen the dovecote to the north and east so that from the house and main lawn only the top section of its roof and the louver are visible giving it an air of mystery which is prolonged as one approaches from the east along a shrub lined path until the dovecote is fully revealed. The path then continues around the dovecote and into the rose garden. This dovecote is highly regarded as an attractive asset, providing interesting cameo views from various parts of the garden.

It is not within the scope of this article to provide descriptions of all the sites visited although it should be noted that at each site the dovecote looked at home in its setting and not at all incongruous, possibly owing to its

Figure 10 The dovecote plays an integral part in this secluded area of the garden at Woolpits.

Figure 11 The south-west view of the Harlow dovecote with the rose garden border alongside the moat.

age, design and architectural proportions. When asked for a personal opinion of how their dovecote fitted into its present setting, several owners felt that 'it is what it is' and suggested that it did not need to be incorporated into a designed garden landscape in order to be appreciated as a valuable feature in its own right. Other owners, whilst

Figure 12: The Harlow dovecote is an integral part of the rose garden.

acknowledging the historical integrity of their dovecote, saw its ornamental potential to enhance the area of garden in which it stood. All the owners interviewed appeared to value their dovecotes and accept the responsibility to look after them. However, one owner did express regret that her impressive red brick dovecote had been constructed in such a position that it partly obscured the view over the valley of the River Pant. Smith shows the dovecote in 1931 as being part of a farm complex but today it stands alone in the centre of the view from the house across to the borrowed landscape. It is the only dovecote visited to still be used by pigeons and they seem to have colonised it of their own volition!

All twelve dovecote sites visited were also recorded by photograph and these were, where possible, of the same view as Smith depicted in 1931. In almost all cases little change had taken place during the last seventy-eight years, although most dovecotes were in better condition than depicted in 1931.

In fact all the dovecotes visited were in reasonably good condition, particularly externally. Most of the dovecotes were being used for storage, partly because some of the owners were unsure of what other use to make of them. One owner, an amateur artist, would have liked to convert her dovecote into an art studio but accepted that the lack of windows restricted the amount of available internal natural light needed to paint. Another owner felt that his dovecote had the potential to be made into separate living accommodation but had not pursued the matter anticipating difficulties in being granted planning consent owing to restrictions linked to its listed status. Two Essex sites that are sometimes open to the public have made good use of their dovecotes: The one at Spains Hall in Finchingfield has been incorporated

Figure 13 A dovecote in the Gestingthorpe area in 1931 (as depicted in Smith's Pigeon Cotes and Dove Houses of Essex, *p191). A photograph from the same position taken in 2009 shows little alteration to either dovecote or surroundings.*

with the adjacent stable block into a wedding venue complex and the one at Easton Lodge near Dunmow is used to display historical information about the Countess of Warwick's former estate.

Conclusion

Dovecotes have been a feature of the rural landscape for centuries and one might wonder why over two thousand have survived countrywide considering that very few now fulfill their original function. The specific requirements of the birds housed within them and the desirability of some original owners to have a prestigious building worthy of their status dictated, to a certain extent, the design of dovecotes. Tending to be comparatively tall in relation to their floor plans, dovecotes have interesting roof shapes, in some cases topped by an ornate weather vane, and they comprise attractive buildings that create a certain presence which enhances the landscape whether designed or not. Land usage around the principal buildings can change over time and some dovecotes have become part of the site's ornamental grounds with their picturesque quality making them an interesting feature and possibly a focal point within such a setting. In these circumstances a redundant dovecote could earn its keep as an ornamental asset. However, some owners may require their decorative dovecotes also to fulfill a practical purpose but, internally, the paucity of windows and the relatively limited floor space does restrict modern usage mainly to that of storage. Fortunately this has the advantage of not affecting the external appearance and, therefore, does not compromise the dovecote's historical integrity.

In the past many probably survived because the

positioning of nest-boxes made it comparatively easy to insert additional floors and so convert redundant dovecotes into dual-purpose buildings that had various practical applications. On the other hand, it seems reasonable to assume that some dovecotes survived, albeit in varying states of disrepair, as a result of their owners' indifference towards them once they were no longer productive. Others may have been spared because very little extra land would have been gained by their demolition, as their floor plans didn't cover much ground.

However a great many dovecotes have been lost over the years and it is fortunate that during the later half of the nineteenth century attention was drawn to some surviving dovecotes with the publishing of a few papers on their historical background. Following this, some county surveys were undertaken including one in 1890 by Alfred Watkins featuring the dovecotes in Herefordshire. McCann suggests that 'The subject only began to impinge on the public awareness with the publication of *A Book of Dovecotes* by Arthur O. Cooke in 1920'.[47] Over two hundred dovecotes throughout parts of England, Scotland and Wales were described in his book and Cooke claims that '.... Essex yields us a good store of dovecotes'.[48] He then goes on to mention eleven of them of which those at Dynes Hall, in Great Maplestead, and Great Bardfield Hall now appear to be lost. Hopefully, the twentieth century introduction of the listing procedure for buildings of historical merit should help to ensure the best possible future for extant dovecotes.

For surely, whether a duffus is used for a specific purpose or allowed to stand empty as a testament to its former glory, we should embrace the fact that so many of these wonderful old dovecotes have survived in the county to enhance the landscape. In the words of G.E. Buncombe:

> 'The Essex "duffus" contributes much towards the beauty and charm of Essex.'[49]

Acknowledgements

The author wishes to thank all the owners who completed the questionnaires and is especially grateful to all those who allowed her to visit their dovecotes. All photographs were taken by the author in 2009 and are reproduced here with the permission of the owners whose dovecotes have been featured.

Please note that all photographs are taken in private gardens which are not open to the public.

The author also wishes to thank John McCann for sharing his knowledge and for providing very useful reading material. The author is also very grateful to Sarah Green and her colleagues at English Heritage for information provided.

The two line drawings included in this article have been taken from Donald Smith's *Pigeon Cotes and Dove Houses of Essex,* Simpkin Marshall, 1931. All reasonable steps have been made to find the copyright holder.

Bibliography (for abbreviations See page 4)

Bond, R., Walker, J. & Andrews D., 2006 'A Medieval detached kitchen at Little Braxted Hall' in EAH, 37, 103-115.

Brunskill, R.W., 1999 *Traditional Farm Buildings of Britain*, Orion Publishing Group Ltd.

Buncombe, G.E., 1999 'Dovehouses and the "duffus" in Essex' in EC, January 1960.

Cooke, A. O., 1920 *A Book of Dovecotes*, T.N. Foulis.

Creighton, O. H., 2009 *Designs Upon the Land - Elite Landscapes of the Middle Ages*, Boydell Press.

Department of the Environment, 1975-1988 *List of Buildings of Special Architectural or Historical Interest in Essex*, numerous volumes covering specific Districts in Essex.

Essex County Council, May 1995 'The Pigeon Mount, Thorndon Park, Brentwood', ECC Field Archaeology Unit Report.

Hansell, P. & J., 2001 *Doves and Dovecotes*, Shire Publishing Ltd.

Jerram-Burrows, L. E., July 1960 'Rochford's Unique Dovecote' in *EC*.

McCann, J., 1991 'An Historical Enquiry into the Design and Use of Dovecotes' in *TAMS*, 35.

McCann, J., 1992 'Dovecotes: An Addendum', in *TAMS*, 36.

McCann, J., July 1995 'The Conservation of Historic Dovecotes', in *JAMC*, 1, No 2.

McCann, J., 1997a 'The Dovecote at Hedingham Castle', in *EAH*, 28.

McCann, J., 1997b 'The Origin of Clay Lump in England', in *VA*, 28.

McCann, J., 2000 'Dovecotes and Pigeons in English Law', in *TAMS*, 44.

Meir, J., 2006 *Sanderson Miller and his Landscapes*, Phillimore.

Roberts, M.D.L. & Gale, V.E., 2000 *Pigeons, Doves and Dovecotes*, Golden Cockerel Books.

Smith, D., 1931 *Pigeon Cotes and Dove Houses of Essex*, Simpkin Marshall.

Smith, D., 1932 'More Essex Dovecotes' in *ER*, 41.

Tusser, T., 1571 (1984) *Five Hundred Points of Good Husbandry*, (Oxford UP edition).

Whitnall, F.G., February 1968 'An Essex Duffus' in *EC*.

Primary Source

ERO: 1/Mb 62/1/6 Photo of oil painting of Bower Hall, c1710

References

1 from a poem by William Barnes, quoted by Cooke 1920
2 Roberts 2000, 51
3 Smith 1931, 7
4 This point was also made by one Essex owner who had invested in some ornamental doves for her newly renovated dovecote and had kept them confined for the advisable period of time, allowing them to settle into their new home, only to release them one morning and watch them heading for the coast – never to see them again! Personal communication with the author 2009
5 Smith 1931, 9
6 McCann 1991, 99-100
7 Hansell 2001, 33
8 Roberts & Gale 2000, 53-54
9 McCann 2000, 27
10 McCann 2000
11 McCann 2000, 31
12 McCann 2000, 35
13 Smith 1931, 69
14 Hansell 2001, 7
15 McCann 1991, 90-97
16 McCann 1991, 95
17 Tusser 1571 (1984), 68
18 Smith 1931,113
19 Hansell 2001, 7
20 Smith 1931, 114-117
21 McCann 1991, 98
22 Roberts & Gale 2000, 59
23 Smith 1932, 178
24 McCann 1991, 97
25 McCann 1991, 134
26 McCann 1991, 125
27 Smith 1931, 246
28 McCann 1991, 109
29 Essex County Council 1995, para 6.0
30 McCann 1997b, 57
31 McCann 1992, 138
32 Smith 1931, 143-263
33 Bond et al, 2006, 103-115
34 Smith 1931, 4
35 Jerram-Burrows, 1960, 244
36 Smith 1931, 170
37 Buncombe 1960, 63
38 Smith 1931, 234-235
39 Hansell 2001, 26-27
40 Meir 2006, 233
41 Hansell 2001, 27
42 Essex County Council 1995, para 2.2
43 Robert Adams provides more information on Pigeon Mount in another article in this publication.
44 Smith 1931, 160-161
45 McCann 2000, 38
46 Personal communication, 2009.
47 McCann 1991, 90
48 Cooke 1920, 157
49 Buncombe 1960, 63

Honey Bees in Essex Gardens

Tricia Moxey

Chase House, Greensted Road, Chipping Ongar, Essex, CM5 9LA

'The bees are hiv'd, and hum their charm,'
Charles Cotton 1630 – 1687[1]

Introduction

This article provides a summary of the history of bee-keeping in England and examines the role of bees within gardens with particular reference to Essex gardens. The article also discusses the various types of bee-shelters or housing used and describes those forms found within historic Essex. It concludes with comments on the general decline of bees and their future in gardens.

History of Bee-Keeping

Honey bees (*Apis mellifera L*) are social insects, living in a colony which is supported by honey stored in wax combs. In the wild, honeycombs can be found inside hollow trees and these are still harvested by honey hunters using traditional techniques. A viable colony of bees will contain a single queen and a number of workers. During the warmer months of the year, the queen will lay up to 2,000 eggs a day in the brood comb, each egg taking three weeks to develop. The larvae will be fed on a mixture of pollen and honey, producing a fresh supply of workers to forage for food. To gather half a kilo of honey an individual honey bee will have to make some 500 foraging trips, sipping nectar from as many as 10,000 flowers, which is why placing hives near flower rich areas is so important. The honey is stored in honey comb, a delicate double sided wax structure. A full honey comb weighs roughly a kilogram and will yield about 68 grams of wax.

In spring, new queen bees and males or drones are raised within the hive and a new colony is created as the bees swarm with the old queen, flying off to found a new colony. A beekeeper might start the year with four colonies, but might have as many as twelve before the onset of winter. An early or prime swarm is more likely to form a successful colony, hence the traditional saying:

A swarm of bees in May - Is worth a load of hay
But a swarm in July - Is not worth a fly.

The size of a swarm is an indication of its strength, sometimes it was measured in pecks or bushels[2] and a really good swarm might be half a bushel in size.

Most foraging by bees is achieved within three to five kilometres of the hive, but having a good selection of flowers near to the hive saves energy. Bees detect odours using their antennae, but are also aware of the different colours of petals and communicate the location of suitable flowers to their co-workers by a dancing wriggle. For centuries beekeepers have recognised that placing hives near flowering trees gave their bees a useful boost in early spring. Favourite nectar producing trees include willow, apple, cherry, hawthorn, lime and sycamore. The sticky antibiotic substance propolis is found on buds of birch, poplar and willow and is collected by bees and used to seal cracks within the hive. The role of bees in pollination was not appreciated until 1750, when Arthur Dobbs wrote about his observations on bees collecting pollen from daisies and fruit trees in his walled garden.[3]

In Europe traces of honey have been found in a Neolithic pottery utensil thought to have been used for brewing mead[4] and bee husbandry was established in Egypt by 2,400 BC.[5] The Romans also kept bees. Virgil (70-19 BC) recommended that in an apiary: 'the bees are to be in a shady corner out of the wind, where sheep, goats and cattle cannot penetrate... Yet water is present, and in it are stones and wood to help the bees to dry themselves'.[6] From early times it was the practice to provide bees with nectar rich sources by growing fragrant flowers such as thyme and marjoram near their hives. Clean water, which is essential for bee health and honey production, should also be placed near to the hive.[7]

Bees can be housed in various containers including, at the most basic, hollowed logs or domed clay pots with an entrance hole. The traditional European bee 'skep' is an inverted basket formed from a continuous coil of straw

Figure 1 *Sketch of traditional bee skep (author's sketch)*

Figure 2 Wildman's Skep with upper collecting box covered with hackle. Five bars inserted in the lower skep give support to the combs. Wildman, Thomas, A Treatise on the Management of Bees, London, 1770.

held together by binding it with a natural string made from bramble or stinging nettle. Rye straw is the preferred material. The basket is either domed or flat topped approximately 38 cm (15") in diameter and 30 cm (12") high, the actual dimensions being determined by tradition and the lap size of the maker. A carrying handle might

be included on the top. Traditional straw skeps were of a sufficient size to accommodate twenty thousand or more bees, which is a viable colony comprising a single queen and an adequate number of workers. Slight variations of the skep were produced including one known as the Chelmsford Skep, which was reputed to be especially well formed.[8] A skep could be placed on a single pole, or on a four legged stool or a raised platform of wood with a landing stage in front of the hive. Straw skeps provide little protection from the elements and were often covered by a straw mat known as a hackle or were sealed with a mixture of cow dung and sand to keep them watertight.

Traditionally, bee colonies were sacrificed in order to collect the honey stored within the honey comb, but a number of beekeepers in the eighteenth and nineteenth centuries designed innovative hives which allowed the bees to be preserved when taking the honey harvest. In his book *The English Apiary* published in 1721, Gedde bemoaned that: 'the ancient form of hives are subject to so many Inconveniences, Charge, Trouble and Casualties'.[9] Gedde set about designing an improvement which consisted of three octagonal boxes standing on top of one another, each with small panes of glass let into the sides so the activities of the bees could be observed.[10] Honey could be gathered from the upper boxes without harming the bees. In the later eighteenth century, Thomas Wildman experimented with fixing a series of seven parallel wooden bars across the top of a 25.6 cm (10") diameter skep on which the bees could fix their comb. The addition of the top skep allowed the bees to use this upper chamber to store honey within fresh comb and this could be easily removed for harvesting without killing the bees.[11] Another design, the Humane Cottage Hive enabled easy collection of honey as the bees filled removable jars with fresh honey comb. Hibberd claims that 'the bees work well in it, it serves well for study, and may be managed with ease by the most timid'.[12]

Other designs included the Nutts Collateral Hive with the wooden boxes side by side. Hibberd suggested

Figure 3 Nutt's Collateral Hive – an imposing structure with glass panels so the activities of the bees can be monitored. Nutt, Thomas, Humanity to Honey-Bees or practical directions for the Management of Honey-Bees, H. & J. Lach, 1834.

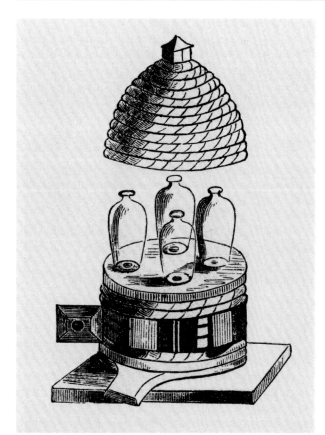

Figure 4 Humane Cottage Hive where the honey comb is formed in removable glass jars. There is a glass panel in the side of the skep so the bees can be observed within it. Hibberd, J. Shirley, Rustic Adornments for Homes of Taste, *Groombridge & Sons, London, 1856.*

that: 'this fanciful hive would make a very appropriate ornament to a Chinese or Italian summerhouse … although for a rustic aspect nothing would be more appropriate than straw hives'.[13] Whilst there were a considerable number of innovative hives available during the nineteenth century, it was Lorenzo Langstroth who, in 1851, realised the significance of the internal bee space between the honey combs. This led to the subsequent development of the moveable frame and the construction of standardised wooden hives. The Langstroth Hive which became commercially available in 1860 is one example, but the cottage style double skinned WBC named after its designer, William Broughton Carr, was also commonly used. The robust, square British National hive is now in general use throughout the United Kingdom. Straw skeps are still used for collecting swarms, but currently it is illegal to keep bees within them as it is impossible to examine the colony for signs of disease.

Garden Bee Structures

Honey bees require ready access to flowers for their source of nectar and pollen. John Fitzherbert's *Book of Husbandry* 1523 is probably the first English writer to give advice about keeping bees in a garden. In the 1534 edition he states: 'It is convenient, that the hyve be set in a garden, or an orchyarde, where as they maye be kepte from the north wynde, and the mouth of the hyve towarde the sonne'.[14] If positioning them near a wall it was important to check what was on the other side. Kilns

or dung heaps should be avoided as bees do not like foul smells or undue noise.

Essex born Thomas Tusser, writing in 1580, describes how a hive should be placed:

> Set hive on a plank, not too low by the ground,
> Where herbs with the flowers may compass it round;
> And boards to defend it from north and north east
> From showers and rubbish, from vermin and beast.[15]

Charles Butler recommends that hives should be 'nigh your home, that the Bees may be in sight & hearing; because of swarming, fighting, or other sodaine happe, wherein they may need your presente helpe'.[16] He also suggest that single stools are best '… set about two foot apart, although they bee laid flat on the ground but it is better to reare them with foure leggs, though little and short'.[17] Gedde recommends that the bee garden be well fenced, especially to the north and west, with the entrance to the hives between a foot and a foot and a half from the ground, facing towards the south east. Water from an overhanging tree or roof must not drip onto them. The area in front of the hives should be short mown grass as bare soil gets wet in winter and dusty in summer.[18] He also suggests that planting and hedging within the garden should include elm and oak and sweet flowers, but he also cautions against having too many colonies of bees.[19]

Some gardens had many hives: John Evelyn notes that on visiting the garden of his kinsman, Sir Robert Clayton: 'All the ground is so full of wild thyme, marjoram and other sweet plants, that it cannot be overstocked with bees; I think he had near forty hives of that industrious insect'.[20] If the number of hives became too large for a small garden, Butler recommended: 'a square green plot fitted for the purpose … sixty three hives be set out in formal rows of nine times seven … which being well ordered, will yield the Bee master the better part of a liberall maintenance; if any be so happy as to attain unto it'.[21]

Figure 5 Ornate Bee House. Hibberd, J. Shirley, Rustic Adornments for Homes of Taste, *Groombridge & Sons, London, 1856.*

Providing shelter for skeps during inclement weather was essential and placing them on shelves within a wooden lean-to was the most likely method of keeping them dry. In many parts of the British Isles more permanent covers for bee colonies were made by creating alcoves or recesses, known as bee boles, within walls. Early examples of these can be found in a garden wall dating from 1490 in Canterbury, Kent.[22] Similar recesses were incorporated into the brick or stone walls of the gardens of large houses: they can be dated using evidence from the surrounding wall.

In 1952, the International Bee Research Association commenced a Register of surviving bee boles.[23] By 1981 550 had been recorded[24] rising to 1,492 in December 2009.[25] Bee related structures occur throughout the British Isles, but more have survived in some counties, e.g. Cumbria 302, Yorkshire 161, Kent 56, Cornwall 55, Northumberland 25, while fewer surviving bee boles were found in Essex 14, Norfolk 13, Derbyshire 11, Sussex 9, Hertfordshire 6, Suffolk 4 and Bedfordshire 3.[26] There are good reasons to provide extra shelter in wetter counties, but it is possible that in some areas local traditions or alternatively a desire for innovation influenced those creating bee boles. Access to local stone for creating walls may also have been an important factor as brick walls were an expensive commodity.

Typically a bee bole is 36 - 46 cm (14 -18") high, 31 - 46 cm (12 -18") wide and 31 - 46 cm (12 - 18") deep set into the wall between 31 - 91 cm (12 - 36") from the ground for ease of handling the skep. The usual size of a skep ensured that it would fit quite snugly within such an alcove. Occasionally bee boles were sufficiently wide to house two or more skeps side by side. Bee boles may occur singly or a number may be inserted along a wall. Sometimes they are double or treble banked. In stone walls they are often rectangular boxes, but many in brick walls have a fine arched top, a lasting testament to the skills of the local bricklayers. Occasionally, they have a triangular top. Most bee boles are located at about waist height but some occur at a greater height. Close fitting wooden shutters gave additional protection in winter.

Bee boles may be created in house walls, in garden walls near orchards or beneath a terrace wall, their number reflecting the importance of hives to the economy of that estate. Many records list properties with ten or more bee boles, but larger establishments had more, such as the National Trust property of Packwood House in Warwickshire, where there are thirty bee boles, dating from 1756, on the south facing side of the terrace.[27] In their paper, the History of Beekeeping in English Gardens, Walker and Crane[28] analysed the records for 759 walls containing such recesses, discovering that seventy four percent face south, south-east or south-west. Fourteen percent face east, six percent face west, with the remainder facing north or north-west.[29] This correlated well with the prevailing wind direction at each site.

The IBRA Register records a few wooden structures used for housing bees all year round. Generally these had three fixed sides and a roof, with a front which could be opened to access the hives within. If sufficiently large, there might be a door in the side. Occasionally more elaborate forms were advertised. In his Rustic Adornments for Homes of Taste Hibberd recommended the rustic design (Figure 5). In this the hives were placed along a shelf on the south side while the north served as a summer house, the hives being enclosed with moveable glass sashes for the purpose of observation.[30] His own was a more modest structure. 'It was a simple shed with a thatched roof, with three rails along the centre for the hives, which are open to view in all directions. In the winter a screen is attached to the north side to protect the hives from the cutting winds'.[31]

Bees could be moved into winter quarters in the form of a wood, brick or stone bee house which has several internal recesses,[32] or they were relocated to cellars, being placed in suitable alcoves. Examples have been identified in a number of properties in Kent[33] and Surrey[34].

Observing Bees

During the seventeenth century, there was increasing interest in bees as social insects. William Mew, Rector at Easington in Gloucestershire drew up a design for an octagonal, glass-sided, beehive before he went away during the Civil War. His wife arranged for one to be installed in his garden to await his return in 1652.[35] The model was passed on to Dr John Wilkins, Warden of Wadham College, Oxford who had one set up in his garden. He in turn gave one to John Evelyn in 1654 who set it up in his garden at Sayes Court in Deptford, Kent where it was viewed by Charles II.[36] This hive was still there in 1665 when Samuel Pepys recorded seeing it on 5th May that year.[37]

Bees were housed within glass beehives at Canons in Middlesex, which was owned by the Duke of Chandos. His wife, Cassandra, had been tutored by John Ray, the Essex natural historian who had considerable interest in entomology, including the activities of honey bees. Keeping bees in such glass hives provided instruction and entertainment for guests. Following his visit to Canons in 1722, James Mackay wrote: 'in the large kitchen garden there are bee hives of glass, very curious'.[38] It is possible that glass hives might have been present in the gardens at Wanstead, the seat of Sir Richard Child, Cassandra's younger half brother – there was some sibling rivalry between the two! Sadly as no records survive this can only be conjecture, as all the Wanstead Estate papers disappeared with the demise of the grand house in the early nineteenth century. However, a neighbour at Aldersbrook, Smart Lethieullier, FRS, a man noted for his wide range of interests, owned one.[39]

Such glass beehives seem to have started a trend as the inclusion of glass within hives is mentioned by several authors of beekeeping manuals. Watching the activities of the hive was recommended as a pastime with the suggestion that a skep should be located within sight of the house so that members of the household might see and hear the bees.

Wandering through their well ordered flower filled gardens, scientists and gardeners such as John Ray, Richard Bradley[40] and others had the opportunity to observe and record the activities of bees as they moved amongst the flowers. Philip Miller in a letter to Bradley in 1721, described his experiments made with tulips and spinach plants in his gardens that proved that it was the 'farina' carried by bees rather than the wind which had impregnated the flowers.[41]

Bees in Essex Gardens

Essex has a reputation as an area suited to successful bee keeping. The Domesday Survey of 1086 lists the possessions of each manor at that date and records the number of apiaries within Essex as 130.[42] The total number of hives within Essex was 612,[43] many more than in other parts of East Anglia: Suffolk had 350[44] and Norfolk 467[45] respectively. The survey only included those hives farmed for the manorial lord and did not include those which provided honey for the villeins or cottars, and there may have been many more.[46]

In 1086, the distribution of hives within the country was uneven, with more being found in the north-west of the county around Saffron Walden, which was more densely populated.[47] Saffron Walden had thirty hives, the manor at Shortgrove, near Newport had twenty three hives, Thaxted had sixteen and Theydon twelve. There were ten hives in the manor of Barking, the location of the important Abbey originally founded 666AD. In total, 35 manors had over five hives, 13 manors owned five hives, 17 manors had four hives, 29 manors had two hives and 11 manors had just one hive. Occasionally, changes in the number of hives were recorded. For example at Tolleshunt Major there had been two hives before 1066 but none were recorded in 1086, and the ten hives at Stanstead had been reduced to eight by 1086.[48] Using the information contained within the Domesday Survey it is possible to estimate of the number of heads of households and this gives a favourable ratio of one officially registered hive to every twenty three families.[49]

A document from Writtle parish dated 1414, records two tenants, William Spryngefeld and John atte Melle, who had the tenancy of a cottage and garden curtilage, their warranty clause stating that they had to provide two wax candles for use in the church and chapel at Christmas. If they supplied the candles from their own hive, they would have needed several hives to keep up the supply. If their bees failed them, the church wardens could enter the property, expel them and let the cottage on a lease to someone else.[50]

Evidence of how many people were actually keeping bees during the twelfth to seventeenth centuries in Essex is scant. Steer found only four references to bees or beehives in his search through 250 surviving inventories, which cover the period 1635-1749.[51] Walker and Crane carried out an analysis of probate inventories from seventeen English counties between 1550 and 1730 which revealed that the average number of hives increased with social standing; on average labourers owned 2 hives, yeoman might have 3.6 and a gentleman 4.4.[52] The records suggest that several Essex beekeepers seem to have held greater stocks of bees as John Dyer of Great Maplestead, husbandman, had eleven hives and several men had as many as nine stocks of bees.[53] Bees might also be willed to others, for example in 1601 Edward James of Stock bequeathed a hive to Joan Harris.[54]

Many Essex beekeepers seem to have kept their hives in yards, where they could be watched for signs of swarming, but they were not always safe as is described in this record in the Session Roll from 1620.

'On February 4 1620, Recognizance of Thomas Gardner husband and Thomas Stocke yeoman, both of Good Easter; Gardner to answer Mrs. Kinge of Roxwell widow, for that, with others in his company, on New Year's day last at night, being in drink, before their coming thither they were shut out of doors and in revenge thereof did destroy certain hives of bees of hers standing in her yard, throwing them into the moat. Unpaid'.[55]

Bees were kept at both of the Petre estates of Ingatestone Hall[56] and Old Thorndon Hall.[57] The Petre acounts record John Hedge as having two hives of Bees and Mary Bentley putting honey into four earthenware pots.[58] A skep is recorded in an inventory of Old Thorndon Hall,[59] but no details are given of where the hives were placed.

Surviving Bee Structures in Essex Gardens

Twenty-three bee related structures have been identified in Essex. Sixteen are included on the Register held by the International Bee Research Association,[60] another five possible locations are listed on the Essex Historic Environment Record[61] and there are two known but, as yet, unlisted sites. One of these is Hassenbrook Hall near Basildon and the other is the wall to the south of the churchyard of St. Margaret's Church, Barking on the edge of the A124, Barking Road. Only two sites are open to the public, the remainder are in private ownership.

The following sites are of particular note.

1. **South Shoebury Hall Farmhouse, Shoeburyness** (near Southend on Sea).[62] Private.

   A possible bee house is located in a garden; it is built of rustic burr bricks and has some very shallow recesses within it. Constructed post 1700.

2. **Moat House, Matching Green.**[63] Private.

   Two large alcoves located facing south east, within the exterior wall of the brick chimney. The alcoves measure 94 cm (37") tall, 56 cm (22") wide and 25.4 cm (10") deep. The height is more than adequate for a single skep. Chimneys of this type were added to earlier buildings in the latter years of the sixteenth century, but as yet no others with similar alcoves have been uncovered.

The following three sites have connections with former religious establishments which were disbanded at the time of the Dissolution.

3. **Tilty Hall Farm, Dumnow.**[64] Private.

   Six arched bee boles are arranged in two rows within a fragment of a mortared flint wall within the farmhouse garden. This wall is 2.4 m (8') long and 1.5 m (5') high with supporting buttresses at the corners. The alcoves themselves are arched and measure 43 cm (17") tall, 61 cm (24") wide and 56 cm (22") deep. The wall is angled so the bee boles face south. These were restored by members of the Essex

Figure 6 Bee bole in wall next to Barking Road (photograph by author).

Figure 7 Bee bole in garden wall, Eastbury Manor (photograph by author).

Beekeepers Association in 1967, the new arches being constructed from hand made bricks.[65] This wall may have been constructed as a separate structure within the grounds of Tilty Abbey.[66]

4. **Wall on site of Barking Abbey, Abbey Road, Barking.** Public.

Two arched alcoves in brick wall, one is in good condition and the other has suffered some damage in the past. The intact alcove measured 40.6 cm (16") tall 36.8 cm (14.5") wide, and 23.5 cm (9.25") deep. Both are 112 cm (44") from ground level. A black deposit, which may be a residue of traffic fumes, is present in both.[67]

5. **The Vicarage, Hatfield Peverel.**[68] Private.

There are seven arched recesses in the surviving sixteenth century brick wall of the former Hatfield Priory. Now bricked up, they measure 63.5 cm (21") high by 83.8 cm (33") wide.

The following sites have a number of bee boles within walls.

6. **Assington Hall, near Colchester.**[69] Demolished.

Three triangular recesses discovered in 1967 after a fire in which the house burnt down. Located in a wall were facing south west, they measured 38 cm (15") high, 38 cm (15") wide and 28 cm (11") deep at a height of 114 cm (45") above the ground. The dimensions of the bricks would suggest a Tudor date for this wall.

7. **Hassenbrook Hall, near Basildon.** Private.

Several arched niches are present in the walled garden and recent analysis by Bulmer Brick and Tile Company has dated the bricks at 1530. There are traces of soot within these niches.[70] This property was built by Sir Richard Champion, who was Sheriff of London in 1530 becoming Lord Mayor in 1565.

8. **Eastbury Manor, Barking.**[71] National Trust.

Six triangular topped bee boles are present in the surviving garden, four in a west facing wall and two in a north facing wall, located 165 cm (65") above ground level. The dimensions are 45.7 cm (18") to the highest point, 30cm (12") wide, 30cm (12") deep.[72] The merchant Clement Sysley (1490 – 1578), built this house and its walled garden in 1557. At that time, the house was surrounded by farmland and orchards lay to the east. Today, the property is owned by the National Trust.

9. **Lambourne Manor House, Abridge.**[73] Private.

There are three arched recesses in the garden wall, measuring 48.2 cm (17") tall, 48.2 cm (17") wide and 25.4 cm (10") deep. The house and garden date from 1571, when it was built by Thomas Barfoot.[74]

10. **Little Wakering Hall, Greenhill, Little Wakering.**[75] Private.

There are two arched recesses in a brick garden wall measuring 58.4 cm (23") tall, 76.2 cm (30") wide, 25.4 cm (10") deep. One faces south and the other west.

12. **North Ockendon Hall Farm, North Ockendon.**[76] Private.

There are two arched alcoves in a brick garden wall which is on the site of sixteenth century moated manor house. They measure 76.2 cm (30") tall, 76.2 cm (30") wide by 30.5 cm (12") deep and face north - north west. This manor was in the ownership of the Poyntz family in the sixteenth century and Sir Gabriel Poyntz (d 1609) was a Sheriff of Essex.[77]

13. **Bretons Manor House, South Hornchurch, London Borough of Havering.**[78] Private.

There are ten arched bee boles located in the walled garden, which is contemporary with the walls of a

16th-century barn.[79] They measure 48.2 cm (17") high, 48.2 cm (17") wide and 25.4 cm (10") deep. At the time of its construction, the house was occupied by the influential Ayloffe family. Sir William Ayloffe was Sherriff of Essex in 1566.[80]

14. **Pond Hall, Wix, Tendring.**[81] Private

Nine arched bee boles in three rows of three in brick wall, facing south east. The wall is dated to pre 1750. The alcoves faced and measured: 40.6 cm (16") high, 40.6 cm (16") wide and 63.5 cm (25") deep.

The rounded brick arch was the favoured form of construction of those bee boles so far identified. But at two sites, Eastbury Manor and Assington Hall, triangular recesses occur. This is a much less common form of bee bole. Two gardens in Hertfordshire have similar examples; one at Much Hadham[82] and the other at Theobalds Place.[83] This type of triangular arch is more common in Kent, being found in a third of the forty-two recorded sites for bee boles.[84] Both arched and triangular shaped recesses have been recorded in the cellar of New Hall, Horsham, W. Sussex.[85] Whilst the majority of bee boles were constructed to house skeps, they might have served other functions. IBRA recorders have noted statues in a few. The presence of soot within the ones at Hassenbrook Hall and Lambourne Hall is intriguing. There is the possibility that they housed lanterns which were lit during frosty nights to protect the blossom of the fruit trees grown on the walls.[86]

The majority of bee boles recorded in Essex date from the sixteenth century and were associated with moderately wealthy sites. Larger properties, such as Copped Hall, Ingatestone Hall, Hylands House and Valentines Mansion, do not appear to have had any permanent bee related structures, although suitable walls may have been demolished.

It is possible that the relative paucity of bee related structures recorded in Essex gardens is due to lack of recognition and recording.[87]

The Future for Bees in Essex Gardens

In the nineteenth century Essex was very rural with well hedged fields and many orchards. Gradually the county has become more urbanised which has had a serious impact on honey production. Production varies from year to year but it is interesting to note the observations of Rev Herbert Brown, rector of Southminster, who in three good seasons between 1881 and 1897 was able to collect an average of 57 lbs of honey.[88] In 1952 the average yield per hive was 37.3 pounds from 1,271 colonies, but the output from one in Clacton was a staggering 290 pounds and one at Chelmsford 250 pounds.[89] In the 1960s there were still 13,000 acres of orchards and 2,000 acres of soft fruit with some 6,000 bee hives in the Essex. By the late 1960s the average yield had declined to 25lbs due to massive changes in the pattern of agriculture, especially the loss of orchards and hedgerows.[90] There has considerable concern about the fate of the honey bee in the UK in recent years with a worrying decline in the number of viable colonies due to disease. Fortunately, as a result of these concerns there is

now £4.3 million of funding, targeted at bee disease surveillance, education and research.[91]

Today, colonies of honey bees are widespread throughout the county of Essex with some 380 registered bee keepers owning one or more hives.[92] Bee hives feature in demonstration gardens such as Hyde Hall (RHS). There are observation hives at the Chelmsford Museum and the Visitor Centre at Bedford's Park, Havering. In the summer of 2009 three new hives were installed in the flower rich garden at Cressing Temple as part of a programme run by Essex County Council to raise public awareness of the importance of bees as pollinators of food crops.[93]

Bees are still an important feature in Essex. Many individual gardeners keep bees within their gardens. Bees are vital for the pollination of many garden flowers and at least seventy crops including apples, pears, raspberries, currants and gooseberries as well as clover, sunflowers, dwarf and runner beans, rape and borage. The welcome addition of 'wild flower' mixes (including bee friendly flowers) on improvements to areas such as road verges, golf courses and flood relief schemes provide food sources for bees, as do 'bee friendly' garden plantings. So giving thought to the location bee hives within gardens and orchards is a vital component of designing a garden!

Acknowledgements

The author is grateful to Penelope Walker for her guidance in sourcing information about bee boles and for access to the IBRA Register for bee boles. The staff at the Essex Record Office have also been of assistance in providing information. Thanks are also due to Richard Oakman, who offered transport and help with some of the measurements. I am also grateful to Fiona Wells for informing me about the bee boles at Hassenbrook Hall and Michael Leach for his guidance.

Bibliography

Altick R.D., 1978 *The Shows of London: A panorama history of exhibitions, 1600–1862*, Belknap Press of Harvard University Press

Atkinson, M., 1999 'Growth and Decay in an Essex Village' in *British Archaeology*, 47

Bagster, S., 1843 *On Bees*, Samuel Bagster and William Pickering

Beresford, J. (ed), 1923 *The Poems of Charles Cotton 1630-87*, New York

Bevan, E., 1843 *The Honey Bee, its Natural History, Physiology and Management*, Philadelphia

Butler, C., 1623 *The Feminine Monarchie - a Treatise concerning Bees and the due Ordering of them*, London

Crane, E., 1999 *The World History of Beekeeping and Honey Hunting*, Duckworth

Darby, H. C., 1971 *The Domesday Geography of Eastern England*, CUP

Dobson, A., 2006 *Diary of John Evelyn 1677 – 1706*, Read Books

Edwards A. C., 1975 *John Petre*, ERO

Edwards, A. C. & Newton, K.C., 1984 *The Walkers of Hanningfield*, Buckland Publications

Ellis, H., 1833 *A General introduction to Domesday*, 1, London

Emmison, F. G., 1991 *Elizabethan Life: Home Work and Land*, ERO

Emmison, F. G., 1987-2000 *Essex Wills: 1563 – 1603*, 1 - 12

Gedde, J., 1675 *A new Discoverie of an excellent Method of Beehouses & Colonies* (reissued in expanded form in two parts in 1721 as *The English Apiary*)

Hartlib, S., 1655 *The Reformed Commonwealth of Bees*, London

Hibberd, J. S., 1856 *Rustic Adornments for Homes of Taste*, London

Huish, R., 1844 *Bees*, London

Lawson, W., 1618 *A New Orchard and Garden with the Country Housewives Garden*, (fascimile Edition with an introduction by Malcolm Thick, 2003)

Lewis, F., 1976 *Essex and Sugar*, Phillimore

Mackay, J., 1728 *A Journey through England*, 2

Miller, P., 1752 *The Gardeners Dictionary*

Morant, P., 1768 *The History and Antiquities of the County of Essex*, 1

Nutt, T., 1834 *Humanity to Honey-Bees or practical directions for the Management of Honey-Bees*, H. & J. Lach

Page, W. & Round, J. H., 1907 *Victoria County History of Essex*, 2

Parker-Pearson, M. (ed), 2003 *Food, Identity and Culture in the Neolithic and Early Bronze Age*. British Archaeology Reports (BAR) International

Powell, W.R. (ed), 1978 *Victoria County History of Essex*, 7

Proctor, M. & Yeo, P., 1973 *The Pollination of Flowers*, Collins

RCHM, 1923 *An Inventory of the Historical Monuments of Essex*, 4, HMSO

Seebolm, F., 1883 *The English Village Community*, Cambridge

Smith, D.A. (ed), 1965 'John Evelyn's manuscript on bees from Elysium Britannicum' in *Bee World*, xlvii

Steer, F. W., 1969 *Farm and Cottage Inventories of Mid Essex, 1639 – 1749*, ERO

Tusser, T., 1580 *A hundred Good points of Husbandrie*, London

Walker, P. & Crane, E., 2000 'The History of Beekeeping in English Gardens' in *Garden History*, 28(2), 231 -261

Wildman, T., 1770 *A Treatise on the Management of Bees*, London

Williams, A. & Martin, G. H. (eds), 2003 *Domesday Book: A complete Translation*, Penguin Classics

Winston, M. L., 1991 *The Biology of the Honey Bee*, Harvard University Press

Wood, E. S., 1963 *Collins Field Guide to Archaeology*, Collins

References

1 Beresford 1923, 55
2 1 peck = 2 gallons =16 pints, 1 bushel = 4 pecks, 1 gallon = 4.55 litres
3 Proctor & Yeo 1973, 24
4 Parker-Pearson 2003, 125 &135
5 Crane 1999, 161
6 Virgil, *Georgics*, IV, 8-12
7 Collumella, *De Re Rustica*, 1st Century AD, IX iv, 4-6
8 Bevan 1843, 34
9 Gedde 1721, 24
10 Gedde 1721, 99
11 Wildman 1770, 94 -95
12 Hibberd 1856, 294
13 Hibberd 1856, 287
14 Fitzherbert 1523,
15 Tusser 1580, 86
16 Butler 1609, ch 2
17 Butler 1609, ch 2 items 12, 13
18 Gedde 1675, 29
19 Gedde 1675, 96.
20 Dobson 2006,10
21 Butler 1623, ch 2 item 1
22 IBRA Register no 375
23 The International Bee Research Association maintains an up to date list of surviving bee boles and related structures.
24 Walker and Crane 2000,
25 IBRA Register, December 2009
26 Data from IBRA Register of Bee Boles updated Nov 2009
27 IBRA Register 15
28 Walker and Crane 2000, 240
29 ibid, 251- 260
30 Hibberd 1856, 288
31 Hibberd 1856, 288 - 289
32 IBRA Register nos 1357,
33 IBRA Register nos 1300, 1301, 1372, 1448
34 IBRA Register no 0162b
35 Hartlib 1655, 47
36 Smith 1965, 119
37 Smith 1965, 199n
38 Mackay 1728, 10
39 ERO D/DSa/158 The author is grateful to the staff of ERO for checking this fact.
40 Richard Bradley FRS was Professor of Botany at Cambridge 1724-1732. He describes his experiments in his *New improvement of Planting and Gardening* published in 1717. He was the gardener at Canons until 1717.
41 Miller 1752, no page numbering. 'Farina' is pollen.
42 Lewis 1976, 3
43 Seebohm 1883, 156
44 Darby 1971,203
45 Ellis 1833, 252
46 As an interesting comparison, in 2009, DEFRA Inspectors checking for bee diseases examined 1529 honey bee colonies in Essex, 1079 in Suffolk and 1578 in Norfolk.
47 Darby 1971, map 53
48 Williams & Martin 2003, 1036
49 Darby 1971, 224-227

50 ERO D/P 50/25/18

51 Steer 1950, 24

52 Walker and Crane 2000, 247

53 Emmison 1991, 30

54 ERO D/P54/1

55 ERO Q/SR 228/85

56 Edwards & Newton 1984, plate XVII

57 Edwards & Newton 1984, plate X

58 Edwards 1957, 74

59 ERO D/DPE2/13

60 IBRA Information for Essex and London Boroughs of Barking and Havering

61 ECC Historic Environment Record

62 IBRA No 1390

63 IBRA No 0876

64 IRBA no 0445

65 Essex Beekeepers Association

66 Lewis 1976, 4

67 Personal observation

68 IBRA no 0904

69 IBRA no 0457

70 Information from Hassenbrook Hall website.

71 IBRA no 0496

72 Personal observation

73 IBRA no .0877

74 Morant 1768, 1, 172 for pedigree of Barfoot family

75 IBRA no 0905

76 IBRA no1359

77 ERO Q/SR 69/2

78 IBRA no 0478

79 RCHM Essex 1923, 4, 73

80 ERO SR17/4446

81 IBRA no 0177

82 IBRA no 0556

83 IBRA Register nos 0556, 1122

84 IBRA Register nos. 0287, 1028, 0471, 0535

85 IBRA Register no 0507b

86 Information from the owner.

87 Recent discussions with two historic building surveyors did reveal that they were unaware of the uses of such structures.

88 Lewis 1976, 7

89 Essex Beekeepers Records 1952

90 Lewis 1976 12 -13 DFERA figs for 1980 list 5,809 acres of orchards and 2,233 acres of soft fruits

91 DEFRA 29 January 2009

92 Essex Beekeepers Association

93 BBC News 28 July 2009

'Tis use alone that sanctifies expense':[1] Cattle, Beauty, and Utility

Ailsa Wildig

Skreens Lodge, Willingale, Ongar, Essex CM5 0SU

Introduction

Cattle are an important and common element of the agricultural scenery in Britain and their needs have partly shaped the countryside in the past and present. Hedgerows were created to be stock-proof and provide some food and shelter for stock, and fields were of a size appropriate to manage a herd of cattle. Cattle are not however just utilitarian, producing milk, meat and other products; but have had an important role in enhancing and beautifying the designed landscape.

Ownership of land, whether predominantly agricultural, pastoral or woodland, has always been a source of status. By the sixteenth century the landscape surrounding large houses was designed for prestige and there was a trend to exclude functional elements from the 'ideal' landscape.[2] By the eighteenth century owning a landscape park was one of the key components of being a member of the landed gentry and within the upper echelons of the 'polite society'. During the first decades of the eighteenth century, the formal landscapes associated with absolutism were largely rejected in Britain, instead there was a shift to a more 'natural' looking design, and landscape parks were designed to resemble a mythical or classical Arcadia. For those with insufficient land or money, the fashion for the ferme ornée combined the functional and the ideal.

The 'agricultural revolution' which intensified from the mid-eighteenth century changed the emphasis for some land-holders back to productivity. The increasing profitability of cattle brought about by the agricultural revolution and the prestige gained from being an agricultural improver was one reason for the shift from deer to cattle within designed parkland from the mid-eighteenth century.

Using a range of source materials, including texts and paintings,[3] this article will examine the role of cattle in the designed landscape. It will explore the appreciation and usage of cattle as landscape elements incorporating utility, beauty and status and also investigate the contribution of cattle, home farms and dairies to the design of the landscape park. The article will commence with an examination of texts which consider the role of cattle in landscape design generally and examine the influence of the portrayal of cattle in landscape painting. It will then focus on Essex examples and conclude with a study of the current role of cattle in the Essex landscape.

'Cattle and Landscape' in Texts and Paintings

The shift to a more naturalistic style of gardening in the eighteenth century was led by the members of the literary and artistic circles. Pastoral landscapes were associated by them with the classical past. Alexander Pope (1688-1744) expresses approval of cattle in the landscape in his Epistle to Lord Burlington (1730-31):

> 'Whose ample Lawns are not asham'd to feed
> The milky heifer..... '

and adds that:

> Tis use alone that sanctifies expense,
> And Splendour borrows all her rays from Sense...[4]

Lady Luxborough, who created a small ferme ornée at her small estate at Barrells Hall, was also a correspondent of the garden writer William Shenstone who had a celebrated ferme ornée at The Leasowes. In 1749 Lady Luxborough wrote to Shenstone: 'Some white pales I have … and fence out the cattle. If they or the sheep come into the front of the Pit, so much the prettier, and they can do no harm'.[5]

In 1782 Horace Walpole described the eighteenth century landscape as a 'painting' using an artist's skills:

> If wood, water, groves, vallies, glades, can inspire or (sic) poet or painter, this is the country, this is the age to produce them. The flocks, the herds, that now are admitted into, now graze on the borders of our cultivated plains, are ready before the painter's eyes, and group themselves to animate his picture.[6]

Humphry Repton (1752-1818), landscape designer, utilised paintings of 'before and 'after' scenes in his famous Red Books, and also within his major written works on landscape design. Repton consciously incorporated cattle, sheep or deer on almost every possible occasion to introduce animation to the landscape and in his sketches.[7] Repton comments on many occasions of the value of objects in motion, in a parkland landscape, and recommended cattle for producing this animation.[8]

> 'A scene, however beautiful in itself will soon lose its interest, unless it is enlivened by moving objects; and from the shape of the ground near most houses, there is another material use in having cattle to feed the lawn in view of the windows.'

He also adds in a footnote:

> 'a large lawn without cattle is one of the melancholy

appendages of solitary grandeur observable in the pleasure grounds of the last century, and is totally incompatible with what might be called park scenery'.

In addition to animation, Repton was also well aware of the importance of the scale of cattle in a landscape.

At Hurlingham, on the banks of the Thames, the lawn in front of the house was necessarily contracted by the vicinity of the river, yet being too large to be kept under the scythe and roller and too small to be fed by a flock of sheep, I recommended the introduction of Alderney cows only; and the effect is that of giving imaginary extent to the place, which is thus measured below a true standard, because if distance will make a large animal look small, so the distance will apparently be extended by the smallness of the animal.[9]

Although primarily concerned with the role of cattle as attractive objects (beauty) Repton was also aware of their utility and profit, working as he so often did with those of the gentry, rather than aristocratic, class. Rogger[10] points out that Repton was well aware that for his more traditional clients 'improvement' had never lost its double meaning of beautification and increased productivity. Referring to Brown and the mistakes of grand landscapes Repton writes:

'When by this false taste for extent, Parks had become enlarged beyond all reasonable bounds of prudence or economy, in the occupation: it then became advisable to allot large proportions of land for the purposes of agriculture within the belt or outlines of this useless and extravagant enclosure, and thus a great part of the interior of the park is become an arable farm. Hence arises the necessity of contracting that portion of an estate in which beauty rather than profit is to be considered'.[11]

Tom Williamson has argued that in the second half of the eighteenth century 'Economic activity lay at the very heart of the landscape park, modifying and in some cases determining important aspects of its structure'.[12] A shift from deer to cattle in parks during the eighteenth century was partly a consequence of the increase in profitability brought about by the 'agricultural revolution' and increasing consumer demand. It was very fashionable for members of the gentry and aristocracy to be seen as active agricultural 'improvers' of both estate and livestock, to such an extent that this was regarded as a patriotic duty. The image of utility and beauty created by the appropriate management of the park emphasised the status of its owner, whilst the very act of cattle grazing in turn created and maintained the much-admired English Landscape style. The browse line created by the trimming of the lower branches by cattle was an important feature of the eighteenth century landscape park[13] as was the short grass grazed by livestock.

By the mid-nineteenth century grazing was much more valuable than arable. In 1801 John Hughes wrote:

'There cannot be more interesting objects of view, in a park, than well chosen flocks and herds, nor more appropriate to the rural scene, than their voices. It is also fit for the lord of the mansion, in the true pride of old English hospitality, to boast the excellence of his beef or mutton, and to be liberal with it.'[14]

J. C. Loudon, (1783 – 1843), a prolific writer on gardening and agricultural improvement, like Repton, was aware of the importance of the size and type of cattle, most especially in his work on suburban gardens. Loudon recommended the keeping of Ayrshire, Guernsey or Alderney cattle in a suburban 'second rate' garden.[15] At Hill House, Saffron Walden, (Essex) George Stacey Gibson, who had a copy of Loudon's *The Suburban Gardener and Villa Companion* (1838) introduced Jersey cattle.[16] Hillyard writing in 1837, advocated the Alderney cow because of their colour. ' No cows, from their generally gay colour, red and white, look so well in a park as these [Alderney cows].'[17] The Jersey Cattle Society describe the breed as small in stature and renowned for its doey eyes and long eye-lashes.[18] At the Repton landscape at Riffhams, Danbury, attractive Jerseys, in scale with the estate size, were introduced by John Charles Spencer-Phillips not long after he moved there in 1908.[19]

Jane Loudon (wife of J.C. Loudon, and herself a prolific garden writer) did not recommend cattle within the park. Writing in 1845 she states 'Cows are particularly destructive to the beauty of park scenery, as they are fond of tearing off the lower branches of the trees and thus producing the hard line which looks as though the branches have been shaved off about five feet from the ground, which is called by landscape gardeners and painters the browsing line'.[20] Where cattle are to be kept she recommends that 'Generally speaking, small, neat, compact-looking cows, are best suited for a gentleman's demesne, as they look better in the landscape, and do not tread up the ground so much as large heavy cattle. Alderney cows are much admired for the elegance of their forms and the richness of their milk, but they are delicate, and are subject to colds and loss of appetite. The Ayrshire cows are quite as handsome, and both better milkers and much hardier; but they are not often to be met with in England'.[21] For the garden writer and landscaper, Beauty, Utility and Profit had become combined in cattle.

A few years after Jane Loudon was writing, Ayrshire cattle did indeed become one of the dominant dairy breeds in Essex. At the end of the nineteenth and beginning of the twentieth century, many dairy farmers from South-west Scotland moved with their Ayrshire cattle to Essex to land which had become derelict because of the agricultural depression. Here, cattle are introduced purely for utility, providing the London market with fresh milk, but add beauty and use to a landscape which had become abandoned.

Paintings[22]

In his *The Artist and the Country House* (1995) Harris discusses a 1679 painting of *The Durdans* (Surrey) by Jacob Knyff.[23] 'The Durdans view announces the consolidation of an English way of looking at a country estate.

We see the Durdans in elevated perspective focusing directly upon the centre of the house and garden with all the variety of estate tasks taking place'. Within this seminal scene there are two black and two brown cattle. These are placed in the middle left of the painting in either an orchard or wood pasture. This area is immediately below the enclosed formal garden and the house is diagonally adjacent to the field with the cattle. This is one of the earliest estate paintings with cattle encountered during the present research. The cattle were presumably included as enhancing the status of the family and their landscape.

Richard Wilson (1714-1782) is widely regarded as 'the founder of English Landscape painting'.[24] Discussing Wilson's 1758 work of Croome Court, Harris notes that: 'When paid by the 6th Earl of Coventry for this canvas in November 1758, Wilson had responded to the first major landscaping commission of Lancelot (Capability) Brown. ... He has transformed Brown's own Mother Nature into a more Arcadian and classical composition'.[25] The painting of Croome includes a cow.

These pastoral landscape paintings were not simply a reflection of the landscape as it was but influenced the way designed landscape would develop.

Another popular genre of painting in the eighteenth century was the allegorical painting. Allegorical portraits depicted the sitter in costumes or settings which contained 'messages' about the sitter or the fashions of the period. Classical and pastoral or rural guises were most popular. One example of this type of painting is the portrait by Charles Jervas, c.1770 of the Duchess of Queensbury shown with milk-maid's pail in hand. The Duchess boasted that she could personally milk a cow. The scene in the background shows milkmaids and their cattle.

Dairies and other farm buildings

The fashionable association between aristocratic women and the pastoral role of the dairy maid in the eighteenth century, was reflected in the importance placed in the building of 'decorative' dairies as part of the designed landscape. Pleasure dairies were one of the few areas in the design of the productive estate where ladies were allowed a significant role. Lady Elizabeth Craven, (1750-1828) the third child of the 4th Earl of Berkeley,[26] was one of the aristocratic women whose wealth and social standing allowed them to take an intense interest in dairies and 'everywhere that Lady Craven went, cows were sure to follow'.[27] She set up dairies in France, Germany and Italy and commissioned John Soane to design garden buildings, possibly a dairy.[28] The third Earl of Hardwicke, a great agricultural improver, also chose Soane to design the farm buildings at Wimpole Hall Farm in the mid 1790s.[29] The Gothic style dairy at Cobham Hall was also re-built about 1790 and moved from its location among farm buildings to a more prominent part of the estate. Repton himself wrote 'The dairy farm is as much part of the place as the deer park, and in many respects more picturesque.'[30]

Cattle and the Landscape in Essex

Utility and Profit: the Agricultural and Estate landscape

Unlike many other counties with reserves of mineral or industrial wealth, agricultural income was a vital source of the revenue of estate owners in Essex, particularly in the late eighteenth century. However, due to the low rainfall in the area, the trend in agriculture in the Eastern Counties has been to specialise in arable rather than livestock farming and cattle farmers in Essex were not generally known for specialist breeding and improvement. Indeed East Anglia (along with north-west Scotland) is currently an area with the sparsest cattle density in Britain (less than 10 per sq. kilometre).[31]

At the end of the eighteenth century, the Board of Agriculture requested reports and submissions throughout the country on the state of agriculture in each county. Messrs Griggs of Hill House, Kelvedon, submitted a detailed report on Essex which included the following:

> Our largest dairy farms are at or in the neighbourhood of Epping, so deservedly famous for the richness of its cream and butter. The farmer even here confines himself to no particular sort of cows, but keeps up a stock of promiscuous cattle, bought in as opportunities offer.[32]

Griggs continues:

> If Essex fails in any part of husbandry, it is in the kind of stock it sends to market, which seem to be brought in without any sort of preference to this or that particular breed. In the course of a few miles ride, you will see North and South Wales, Irish and most other sorts of cattle; ... and it is to be hoped that an instant agricultural society, established within a twelve month under the patronage of our worthy representatives, will tend to correct this great error, and be of very essential service to the interest of the farmer, in all other particulars capable of improvement.

Unsurprisingly, the ferme ornée, dependent on an appreciation of the combination of beauty and utility of livestock, has no noted examples in Essex, although the 8th Lord Petre, of Thorndon (Essex),[33] advised Phillip Southcote who created one of the first ferme ornées at Woburn Farm, Surrey. There are also no nationally recognised Essex painters of livestock.

Beauty: Cattle and the Repton Landscape in Essex

Drawing on the evidence of Repton's Red Books, and his publications on landscape design (illustrated with examples drawn from these Red Books), the Essex Gardens Trust[34] identified the following pictorial examples of cattle within sites where Repton was believed to be involved:

Auberies, Bulmer, Braintree: *The Polite Repository*, 1811 (probably by Repton) and an engraving of Auberies, after 1811 from *The Ladies Memorandum Book* both show cattle and water.

Figure 1 Catherine Hyde, Duchess of Queensbury (after Charles Jervas). (Photo © English Heritage Photo Library.)

Dagnams, Romford: Repton removed the utilitarian fence designed to keep the cattle from spoiling the banks, planted out the banks, and replaced a small section with a 'water fence', which allowed the cattle access to a gravel bottomed platform within the pond. This addressed the problem of cattle poaching the banks of water features and the cattle muddying the water.

Guy Harlings, Chelmsford: has cattle between the house and water in an engraving in *The Polite Repository* again probably by Repton.

Higham Hill (Highams), Walthamstow: Repton's 1793 Red Book shows cattle by the house and deer by the more remote boat-house/pavilion. The 1798 engraving in *The Polite Repository* shows no cattle while the 1810 version does have cattle. Deer from the forest are to be excluded by a sunk fence in the lawn between the house and the water. Here, as in many estates deer are now being deliberately excluded from the parkland and cattle recommended.

Riffhams, Danbury: One of the sketches by Humphry and John Adey Repton, illustrating the views from the new house, depicts cattle.

Spains Hall, Finchingfield: Cattle appear near the house by the edge of the water in a watercolour by John Adey Repton.

Stubbers, North Ockenden: The 1804 *Polite Repository* engraving has three cattle under a tree, and cattle are introduced to the after sketch in Repton's 'Red Book' for this site.

Woodford Hall, Woodford: the 'After' painting includes cattle.

In contrast to the large number of cattle shown in Repton's work in Essex, deer are only seen at the extensive estate of Wanstead, by the boat-house at Highams and at Albyns (Stapleford Abbotts) where Celia Fiennes commented on the park full of deer. There are fewer depictions of sheep than cattle and they are generally on smaller estates. For Repton and his clients in Essex, cattle are the preferred animal for parkland.

Figure 2 Audley End from the West, by Edmund Garvey, 1782 (From the private collection of Lord Braybrooke, on display at Audley End House, Essex. Reproduced courtesy of Lord Braybrooke. Photo © English Heritage Photo Library.)

Figure 3 Audley End and the Ring Hill Temple c1788 by William Tomkins. (Photo © English Heritage Photo Library.)

Cattle in Essex Paintings

In addition to the evidence for cattle in designed landscapes of Essex as portrayed in the works of Repton, there are some paintings of Essex designed landscapes with cattle prominent. Few of these are on public show, but there are several known examples in private collections.[35]

At Audley End, there are several surviving eighteenth century paintings of the estate, with at least three having cattle in the foreground. The painting likely to be the earliest[36] (but not reproduced here) shows cattle, not very accurately depicted.

The painting by Garvey (1782) shows rough coated cattle in the manner recommended by the picturesque writer Gilpin.[37] By the time of the c1788 painting the cattle are depicted much more accurately. They appear to be Shorthorns, the most popular breed of the time. Later records of the nineteenth century (from Hill House, Saffron Walden, Essex) record a Jersey bull at Audley End 'servicing' the dairy cow at Hill House.

A painting by J.T. Selwyn of Down Hall, Hatfield Heath, shows cattle in the foreground, whilst a similar one by the same artist shows sheep instead (private collection). A charming watercolour of Gosfield Hall with cattle in the foreground is in a further private collection. It is likely that many more paintings of estates with cattle survive in private ownership. The presence of animals in the foreground may indicate pride of the owners in their livestock, and sometimes the house is relegated to background detail.

One of the few other paintings of Essex estates with cattle is Constable's painting of Wivenhoe Park (Colchester) (1816). Interestingly, estate paintings of the prestigious property of Copped Hall (Epping) show mainly deer, although they did have Devon Red cattle.

The painting of individual livestock was a popular genre in the late eighteenth to mid-nineteenth century, the period of the 'agricultural improver'. John Vine of

Figure 4 Down Hall, by J. T. Selwyn 1789. (Private collection.)

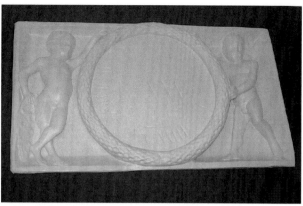

Figure 5 1903 Plaque in Ellen Willmott's dairy commemorating the visit of Queen Alexandra to 'open' the dairy in 1903. (Photograph Ailsa Wildig 2007)

Colchester was a local Essex painter of livestock.[38] Born in c1808, Vine made much of his living by painting prize-winning livestock at agricultural shows as well as at the national fatstock Smithfield Shows. Most of Vine's live-stock paintings have general scenery of trees and water as a background but a few paintings depict the home of the owner of the livestock. One good example of this is the 1843 painting of Lord Western's Devon Ox with Felix Hall, Kelvedon, in the background.[39]

Cattle and Architecture in Essex: Dairies and Home Farms

Essex land-owners, like those of other counties were involved in patriotic agricultural development of Home Farms, such as Hatch Farm, Thorndon (between 1732 and 1778). Frederick Chancellor, renowned Essex and London architect designed covered homestalls, piggeries and a covered homestead for T. W. Bramston of Skreens (Roxwell) in 1861[40] presumably for the Home Farm at Tye Hall. By the time of the 1914 sale of Skreens, there were no buildings for cattle by the mansion. The surviving buildings for cattle at Tye Hall are in Chancellor's style. On prestigious estates it was common to choose a well-known architect to design the farm buildings, a reflection of the status of the owner.

At Skreens (Roxwell) there is cartographic evidence that the 'Milking Yard', Cowhouses, and cattle them-selves were retained in the vicinity of the main house well

Figure 6 Gate piers at Audley End. (Photograph by Fiona Wells)

into the seventeenth century, with cattle, rather than deer, perhaps being kept within the park.[41]

At Warley Place, Brentwood, an ornamental dairy was created at the beginning of the twentieth century. Frederick Willmott purchased land opposite Warley Place in 1882.[42] Here the dairy was developed with an attractive interior, probably by his daughter the accomplished plants-woman Ellen Willmott. In the 1935 Warley Place sales particulars[43] the farm and dairy are described as: 'Farm house built in Swiss style containing on the lower floor a kitchen, scullery and large larder. On the ground floor there is a large model dairy with marble floor and oak inner and outer doors'. Rose Willmott (sister of Ellen) was connected by marriage to the Berkeley family, which had included in the eighteenth century Lady Elizabeth Craven (nee Berkeley), whose interest in dairies is discussed earlier in the article. The dairy at Warley Place contains a plaque reputedly commem-orating the visit of Queen Alexandra to 'open' the dairy in 1903. Ellen Willmott evidently considered the dairy so prestigious that she invited Queen Alexandra to open her dairy as well as visit her garden. The marble dairy shelves remain within what is now an attractive octagonal family dining room, with decorative niches and ornate doors. An old photograph of Warley Place, believed to have been taken before 1934, shows hay being made in the field in front of the house. This field is separated from the turning circle by a ha-ha and this would suggest that livestock would have been seen grazing in the field opposite the front door.

The model dairy at Audley End is adjacent to the house, whereas the stables and other farm buildings are much further away. Cattle played a prominent role in the landscape at Audley End. In the eighteenth century, the East Park was sub-divided into reserves for cattle, deer and partridges.[44] At the Cambridge entrance, the gate piers include bulls' heads, a device taken from the owner's (the Neville family) coat-of-arms.[45] Cattle were originally introduced to coats-of-arms to 'signify the family were land-owning gentry.'[46] In 1811, the polled Yorkshires at Audley End were sold, and replaced by a herd of Alderney cattle. The bull was bought for £429 14s, a very substantial amount of money. These animals provided the foundation for the Jersey herd at Audley End, recognised as the oldest in the country.[47] Successive Lords Braybrooke took great pride in the Jersey herd. They were first shown by the 3rd Lord in 1833, and again at the Royal Society Show in Cambridge in 1840. In the 1880s the Braybrookes kept both Jerseys and Shorthorns, the Jerseys for prestige and beauty, the Shorthorns for profit. Estate records for 1880 –1881 show the labour and feeding costs and have sufficient detail to give the annual value of manure per cow at twice the weekly labour cost per cow (1s 5d).

Cattle in the Modern Essex Landscape

In the twenty-first century pastoral farming in Essex is relatively unprofitable compared to arable farming, so very few cattle still add beauty and utility to Essex estates and the Essex landscape. At Tye Hall (the Home Farm for Skreens) the Shorthorn dairy herd developed into a

Figure 7 Cattle in the parkland at Crix, Hatfield Peverel, Essex

Friesian herd during the seventies but this herd was sold in 1984. In the late nineties Tye Hall was one of the first ten farms in Essex to use cattle in maintaining some of its permanent pasture under the Countryside Stewardship Scheme.[48] Soon after Tye Hall changed ownership in 1998, cattle ceased to graze the pasture by Roxwell brook. At Skreens Park Farm (a new farm developed on Skreens Park parkland), the Friesian dairy herd was sold in 1957 and the last cattle on the parkland of Skreens were the beef-herd of Simmentals in 1987.[49] There are now only about two dozen cattle in the parish of Roxwell, these being kept on one farm, primarily for showing. This is in strong contrast to the 405 cattle recorded on twenty-one farms in the parish in 1916.[50] The animals which now animate Roxwell parish are the trendy alpacas (about two dozen) and leisure horses, with 126 recorded in 2002.[51]

At Crix, there were cattle in the park and circuit field from 1958 to about 1980. Later, Lord Rayleigh's Farms grew arable crops. In the late 1990s the land was returned to pasture under the Countryside Stewardship Scheme.[52] The parkland and circuit field at Crix are currently grazed by Aberdeen-Angus cattle. These cattle are bred for a premium beef market where quality is the driving force, not price. Aberdeen-Angus cattle also now graze land near Leez Priory supplying the same high quality market. At Langleys, Great Waltham, where Repton advised before 1803[53] cattle were still grazing the parkland in 2009.

At Warley Place the meadows beyond the original ha-ha have been managed by the Essex Wildlife Trust since 1999, and cattle graze this and another meadow to the west. The cattle are introduced after the foliage of the many spring bulbs has died down and their purpose is to keep the grass down and allow the spring bulbs, particularly *Crocus vernus* to thrive. The limited amount of grazing and its poor value means this is not a very profitable enterprise. In the last 10- 15 years this movement towards conservation grazing has increased dramatically. In the past many Wildlife Trusts, including Essex,

Figure 8 Cattle at Warley Place, Brentwood, Essex (photograph Ailsa Wildig)

Figure 9 *A Longhorn cow grazing in Epping Forest. (Courtesy of K. French.)*

thought that it was possible to manage grassland through mechanical methods alone, usually through a combination of hay making and autumn cutting to mimic aftermath grazing. Now they accept that grazing plays a key role in maintaining and improving grasslands for both flora and invertebrates.[54] Other landscapes in Essex where cattle are used to graze the landscape primarily for habitat management are Epping Forest where Longhorn cattle are used to conserve the ancient wood-pasture and Hatfield Forest where cattle for many years have maintained the wood pasture which has evolved since Hatfield was a royal 'Forest' with its deer park.

In the twenty-first century, Wildlife Trusts throughout the country manage many previously designed landscapes. In county Durham there were 26 historic sites protected by environmental policies[55] and in Northumberland the Wildlife Trust managed two Capability Brown landscapes in 1997.[56] Where such sites contained pastoral landscapes, cattle still have a role to play for beauty and utility, if not profit!.

Conclusion

The role of cattle changed from purely agricultural to partly decorative during the early eighteenth century. Pastoral farming was still profitable in this era so it was possible to combine beauty with a commercial enterprise by designing parts of the park to contain cattle. Although not a county rich in cattle farming or livestock breeding, Essex contained examples of designed landscapes where cattle were used to effect for the enhancement of landscape as well as status. Cattle in the Essex landscape were rarely however a particular breed. Agriculture, landscape, and social values have changed much since the creation of landscape parks in the era of Polite Society and the role of cattle in adding beauty or utility to a landscape has also changed. None of the Essex landscapes where Repton was known to have recommended or portrayed cattle now contain cattle (as far as can be ascertained). Instead cattle now play an increasingly vital role in successfully maintaining environmentally rich habitats in heritage landscapes: *'Tis use alone that sanctifies expense'* but usage may take many forms!

Bibliography

Briggs, N., 1999 *John Johnson, 1732- 1814 Georgian Architect and County Surveyor of Essex*, Essex Record Office

Cosgrove, D. & Daniels, S., 1988 *The iconography of landscape*, Cambridge University Press

Cowell, F., & Green G., (eds), 2002 *Repton in Essex*, privately printed by Essex Gardens Trust

Daniels, S., 1999 *Humphry Repton: Landscape Gardening and the Geography of Modern England*, Yale University Press

Darley, G., 1999 *John Soane. An Accidental Romantic*, Yale University Press

Davies, J., et al. (eds), 2008 *The Welsh Academy Encyclopaedia of Wales*, University of Wales Press

DEFRA, 2008 *The Cattle Book*, DEFRA

Du Prey, P.R., 1987 'Eight Maids a Milking' in *Country Life* 5 Mar 1987,120-122.

Du Prey, P.R., 1987 'Queens of Curds and Cream: Ornamental Dairies and their Owners' in *Country Life* 181, 104-105.

Ellis, A., 2006 *Oil Paintings in Public Ownership in Essex*. Public Catalogue Foundation

Grant, J., (no date) *Essex Historical, Biographical and Pictorial*, The London and Provincial Publishing Co.

Griggs, Messrs, 1794 *General View of the Agriculture of the County of Essex*, printed by C. Clarke of London

Groves, L., 2002 Animals: Living Garden Features, Not Incidental Occupants, unpublished MA Garden History Dissertation

Harris, J., 1995 *The Artist and the Country House*, Sothebys

Hillyard, C., 1837 *Practical Farming and Grazing*, T. E. Dicey, Northampton

Hindle, P., 1998 *Maps for Historians*, Phillimore

Hodgetts, J. (ed), 1775 *Letters written by the Late Honourable Lady Luxborough to William Shenstone Esq.*, J. Dodsley

Hunt, J.D., 1992 *Gardens and the Picturesque*, MIT Press, London

Hunter, J., 1985 *Land into Landscape*, George Godwin

Jackson-Stops, G., & Pipkin, J., 1988 *The Country House Garden, A Grand Tour*, Pavilion Books, London

Jellicoe, G. & S., Goode, P. & Lancaster, M., 1986 *The Oxford Companion to Gardens* Oxford University Press

LeLievre, 1980 *Miss Willmott of Warley Place*, Faber and Faber, London

Loudon, J., 1838 *The Suburban Gardener and Villa Companion*, Longman, Bowman, Green & Bowman

Loudon, J., 1845 *The Lady's Country Companion*, Longman, Bowman, Green & Bowman

Mason, A.S., 1996 'An Upstart Art: Early Mapping in Essex', unpublished essay in ERO T/Z 438/2/1

Repton, H., 1803 *Observations on the Theory and Practice of Landscape Gardening including some remarks on Grecian and Gothic Architecture*, Bensley

Repton, H., 1806 *An enquiry into the Changes in Landscape Gardening: to which are added some observations on its theory and practice including a defence of the art*, Taylor

Rogger, A., 2007 *Landscapes of Taste, The Art of Humphry Repton's Red Books*, Routledge

Roxwell Revealed 1993, *An Anthology of Village History*, Roxwell Revealed Group, Chelmsford

Roxwell Revealed 2005, *More Roxwell Revealed, A Further Anthology of Village History*, Roxwell Revealed Group, Chelmsford

Scantlebury, H., 2008 *John Vine of Colchester, An account of the life and times of an Essex livestock painter*, Hugh Scantlebury

Stroud, D., 1962 *Humphry Repton*, Country Life

Sutherill, M., 1995 *The Gardens of Audley End*, English Heritage

Wildig, A., 1997 Wildlife in Historic Landscapes, unpublished Architectural Association thesis

Williamson, T., 1993 'The landscape park: economics, art and ideology' in J*ournal of Garden History*,13, 1/2, 49-55

References

1   Epistle to Lord Burlington 1730-31, quoted in Sutherill 1995, 24

2   Hunter 1985, 72

3   Cosgrove & Daniels 1988, 1

4   Epistle to Lord Burlington 1730-31, quoted in Sutherill 1995, 24

5   Hodgetts 1775, letter xli, 165

6   Groves 2002, 32

7   Much readily available work has been written by Repton and about him, for example Daniels 1999, Rogger 2007 and Stroud 1962

8   Repton 1806, 101-102

9   Repton 1803, 6

10 Rogger 2007, 44

11 Repton 1806

12 Williamson 1993, 51

13 Jackson-Stops & Pipkin 1988, 215

14 Williamson 1993, 52

15 Loudon 1838 549

16 Letter from Menell (16/5/1834) in the Victorian Study Centre, Saffron Walden library

17 Hillyard 1837, 52

18 Correspondence with Jersey Cattle Society, 13th August 2009.

19 Grant (no date), (no page number)

20 Loudon 1845, 192

21 Loudon 1845, 281-282

22 A concise early history of landscape and country house painting is given by John Harris in the introduction to *The Artist and the Country House* (1995)

23 Harris 1995, 40

24 Davies 2008, 966

25 Harris 1995, 96

26 Wikipedia

27 Du Prey 1987,104-105

28 Ibid,104

29 Darley 1999, 104

30 Repton 1806, 31-32

31 DEFRA 2008, 6

32 Griggs 1794, 13

33 Jellicoe, Goode, & Lancaster 1986, 529

34 Cowell & Green 2002

35 Ellis 2006

36 Dated by Gareth Hughes (English Heritage) as post c1770 but prior 1784.

37 Hunt, 1992, 5-9

38 Scantlebury 2008

39 Scantlebury 2008, 58

40 ERO. D/F 8/119

41 ERO D/DXa20 and D/DXa21

42 LeLievre, 1980, 46

43 ERO Sale Cat. B921

44 Sutherill 1995, 15

45 Ibid, 10

46 Pers. comm. Myra Wilkins, Heraldry lecturer

47 Pers. comm.. Property manager Audley End

48 Roxwell Revealed Group 1993, 173

49 Pers. comm., Robert Webber, owner

50 ERO, Essex War Agricultural Committee Census Forms, Dec. 1916

51 Roxwell Revealed 2005, 51

52 Pers. comm., Charlotte Wood, owner 1958-2006

53 English Heritage Register of Parks and Gardens

54 Smart, Lisa, Essex Wildlife Trust Reserves Manager, pers. comm

55 Wildig 1997, 9

56 Ibid, 11

Historic Aviaries and Menageries : A Brief History and Some Essex Examples

Jill Plater

Holbrooks, Thoby Lane, Mountnessing, Brentwood, Essex CM15 0TA

'For aviaries, I like them not, except they be of that largeness as they may be turfed, and have living plants and bushes set in them; that the birds may have more scope, and natural nesting, and that no foulness appear in the floor of the aviary'
(Francis Bacon *Of Gardens* 1625)

Introduction

Aviaries and menageries are important elements in gardens and designed landscapes. This article will look at the history of these in general before then focussing on examples in Essex. Aviaries have been a decorative feature of gardens in all parts of the world since ancient times. Sometimes they were constructed of such materials as bamboo, but the majority were of iron, and survivors of these from the past illustrate intricacies of the iron-worker's craft. Apart from being a decorative feature of gardens, the birds in aviaries provided entertainment as well as being a source of scientific interest. Animals were thought to enhance the landscape and the choice of animals was often for picturesque reasons. In the early days of aviaries and menageries the fatality rate was high among the animals and birds as they were caged up for long periods of time whilst being transported often being fed only bread and water.[1] Many of the eighteenth century menagerie owners were interested in naturalising animals shipped here from foreign countries and, of course, having a menagerie of exotic animals was a status symbol as well as being for the pleasure of the house guests. Both aviaries and menageries are discussed in this article as they are closely linked: a building was sometimes called a 'menagerie' in the eighteenth century although it housed only birds. Documentation does not exist for many Essex menageries although 'menagerie wood' on Ordnance Survey maps in some locations suggests the existence of an animal collection at some time.

Early History of Aviaries

The first aviaries that were recorded were created by the Romans, who called them *ornithones*. Marcus Terentius Varro (116-27 BC), the historian, in his treatise *De Re Rustica* (c.40B.C.), does not describe a villa-garden in full but mentions in passing several rich and elaborate gardens which existed in his time. In book III he discusses 'the science of villa-husbandry', which he divides into – 'the aviary, the hare-warren, and the fish-pond'. When he comes to aviaries, he separates them as those designed for profit, and those which are 'merely for pleasure'. This second kind Varro built as part of his own villa near Casiinum, and is described in minute detail. He wrote that square aviaries flanked the entrance, and the double circle of colonnades was enclosed with hemp nets and filled with birds of every species. The domed building in the centre was used as a dining hall where guests were seated around a revolving table and could watch and listen to the birds and look through the net to the countryside beyond.[2]

Varro described the aviary as standing near the bank of a stream, along which

'... runs an uncovered walk 10 feet broad; off this walk, and facing the open country is the place in which the aviary stands, shut in on two sides, right and left, by high walls. Between these lies the site of the aviary, shaped in the form of a writing-tablet with a top-piece, the quadrangular port being 48 feet in width and 62 feet in length, while at the rounded top-piece it is 27 feet. Facing this, as if it were a space marked off on the lower margin of the tablet, is an uncovered walk with a plumula (façade) extending from the aviary, in the middle of which are cages; and here is the entrance to the courtyard. At the entrance, on the right side and the left, are colonnades in the middle with dwarf trees; while from the top of the wall to the architrave the colonnade is covered with a net of hemp, which also continues from the architrave to the base. These colonnades are filled with all manner of birds ... chiefly songsters, such as nightingales and blackbirds.'[3]

Pietro Crescenzi of Bologna wrote a book on husbandry early in the fourteenth century in which he describes the larger gardens of the wealthy as being enclosed with a high wall. 'Towards the north', says Crescenzi, 'there should be a thicket of tall trees where wild beasts are kept and to the south a palace with shady trees and an aviary.'[4] Pietro Crescenzi also wrote of a kind of house for birds 'having a roof and walls of copper wire finely netted'.[5] In 1450 Leon Battista Alberti designed the Villa Quaracchi on the outskirts of Florence to include arbours of evergreens, an aviary and a rose garden.[6]

In the fifteenth century explorations of new or distant countries discovered many rare and beautiful birds to the delight of the avid collectors of Western Europe, and by the sixteenth century the aviary had become a popular and important feature of the garden. Aviaries came in all shapes and sizes, depending on the rank and wealth of the owner. Early Chinese aviaries were of bamboo, whole or split.

Lord Robert Dudley, Earl of Leicester, created a garden and aviary at Kenilworth Castle in his attempts to impress and woo Queen Elizabeth I on her visit of July 1575. The aviary, placed prominently within the garden was 20 feet high, 30 feet long and 13 feet broad and housed pheasants, guinea fowl and old-fashioned canaries. Robert Dudley's usher, Robert Laneham, described the aviary as being 'beautified with great diamonds, emeralds, rubies and sapphires ... and garnished with gold'.[7]

A magnificent garden with aviary was also constructed at Canons in Middlesex for James Brydges in c.1720. Brydges did everything in stupendous style and imported barrow ducks, storks, wild geese, and cherry trees from Barbados, and whistling ducks and flamingos from Antigua. There were also ostriches, blue macaws, Virginia fowls and songbirds, and eagles which drank out of special stone basins.[8]

In *Chinese influences in European Garden Structures*, Eleanor Von Erdberg Consten wrote that 'keeping rare and beautiful birds in a gorgeous cage has always been a favourite pastime of the great and mighty ... the late eighteenth century extended this privilege to the well-to-do bourgeois class. It was quite natural to build in an exotic style for exotic birds – though on a small estate the cage was probably more exotic than its inhabitants'. The pattern books of the period were filled with many styles: rustic, Gothic, Hindu-Gothic, chinoiserie, and rococo'.[9]

Still in existence is the large aviary at Waddesdon Manor, Buckinghamshire, c.1880, which consists of a central pavilion containing rock-work statuary and mosaic flooring and two flanking ranges each of which terminates in a smaller pavilion. It is constructed partly of stone and brick but mainly of wrought and cast iron, much of the latter of elaborate rococo design.[10] Garden aviaries decreased in popularity in the later nineteenth century and later aviaries were built only by those with a sincere interest in birds. Although as Shirley Hibberd wrote in his *Rustic Adornments* 'It must be confessed, that an Aviary is an expensive luxury, whether on a large or small scale; but the lover of birds may do much to gratify his taste without the necessity of a heavy outlay'.

Early history of menageries

Menageries in Europe were surprisingly commonplace and quite often contained large collections of exotic animals from around the world. In later years many of them became public zoological gardens but in the beginning they were status symbols reflecting the owner's wealth and power. Henry I in c.1110 was the first English monarch to keep a private collection of exotic animals in a menagerie. It was situated at Woodstock, which is now within the grounds of Blenheim Palace. He collected lions, leopards, lynxes and any animals that could not be found in this country. During the thirteenth century King John, who reigned in England from 1199-1216, formed a collection of animals at the Tower of London and is known to have held lions and bears. Recently two lion skulls unearthed at the Tower of

London have been dated to Medieval times, shedding light on the lost institution of the 'Royal Menagerie'.[11] By 1710 the collection had grown to more than 280 animals, with hyenas, tigers, seals, camels and baboons. It closed in 1835 and the animals were moved to the new Zoological Society Garden in the corner of Regents Park.[12] James I had a menagerie of birds in St James's Park, including cormorants and ospreys, while Charles II added pelicans, storks, a gannet and cranes.[13]

During the eighteenth century many landowners in Britain were building private menageries and aviaries in the parks of their country estates, using them to show off a range of animals and birds for the pleasure of their house guests.[14] Menageries were sometimes sited at the edge of a park, sometimes near the kitchen garden, sometimes on an island or beside a lake.[15] The 2nd Duke of Richmond (who succeeded his father in 1723) added to the grounds of Goodwood with buildings, trees and animals. His menagerie was situated in Highwood in Goodwood's Pleasure Gardens and the Duke collected wild beasts and birds from all over the world, including wolves, tigers, a lion, jackal, foxes, vultures, eagles, kites, owls, monkeys, racoons, bears, etc.[16] The Dukes of Bedford also created a menagerie at Woburn Abbey, while the 6th Duke of Devonshire had a collection at Chiswick which included emus, kangaroos, Indian cattle, elks, goats, a giraffe and an elephant. The Duke's great stove or conservatory at Chatsworth also included a fine collection of tropical birds.

Some menagerie owners were so proud of their animals that they had them captured on canvas by some of the leading artists of the day, one of whom was George Stubbs, who in 1762-3 painted a zebra that belonged to Queen Charlotte and a lion owned by Lord Shelburne.[17]

Essex Aviaries and Menageries

There is little documented material on Essex aviaries and menageries, although there are passing references to several. The best recorded aviary in Essex was at Audley End and the best recorded menagerie at Thorndon Hall.

Audley End Aviary

The aviary at Audley End was originally constructed in 1774, with later nineteenth century Victorian additions such as dormer windows and barge boards. The aviary was designed by John Mose, a carpenter who worked at Audley End, and it was built in the Gothick style.[18] Within the building were a kitchen, keeping room, and a tea room; the tea room looking into the adjoining aviary. The keeping room housed songbirds in small cages and wild birds such as linnets, yellowhammers and gold-finches. This room was the full height of the building with half a roof, the other half had a blind system that could be opened in fine weather. In the rooms over the tea room the keeper could watch over the birds from a window which overlooked the keeping room. The keeper was unable to look down on the visitors in the garden as the first floor rooms had only skylights. Visitors took tea in the tearoom, which was furnished with four painted chairs, four stools, a mahogany circular table, an Indian matt, a shagreen writing case, twelve silver spoons, one pair of tongs, one strainer, tea pots, cups and saucers, a hand bell, tea chest and several books. Tea was made in the kitchen with its large fireplace with bread oven and water drawn from a well. From the tearoom visitors were led through a glade into the enclosure defined by a star shape representing the Starberry[19] aspect of Warren Hill.[20] Sir John Griffin Griffin had erected a high paling fence to enclose an area of just over seven acres and this was replaced in the nineteenth century with a 2.4 metres high brick and flint wall. Pheasants were kept around the boundary wall and were accessed by a circular path. Many examples of the different species of pheasants were kept in separate units for preservation and to prevent inter breeding. Fantail doves, fancy pigeons, peacocks and many other species of birds would also have been kept in this enclosure.[21] Two golden eagles belonging to the aviary died here, but were preserved and are still displayed in Audley End house. Over the years many of the inmates of the aviary were to achieve posterity when they were incarcerated in glass display domes, becoming part of the important natural history collection at the house.

In his *Tour in Germany, Holland and England* 1826 Prince Herman L.H. Von Puckler Muskau writes of visiting the menagerie at Audley End in October 1826 and how

> 'After many windings, the path brought me under a most lovely leafy canopy, before the ivy covered door of a little building adjoining the gamekeeper's house. This door opened from within, and most enchanting was the view. We had entered a little open saloon, the isolated pillars of which were entirely covered with monthly roses, between them a large aviary filled with parrots on the right and on the left an equally extensive habitation for canaries, goldfinches and other small birds; before us lay an open grass plat dotted with evergreens. The keeper called together 'perfect clouds' of gold, silver, and pied pheasants, fowls of exotic breeds, tame crows, fancy pigeons and other birds, which thronged together in a most gay and motley crowd.'[22]

William Travis was the gamekeeper responsible for the birds, he lived at the aviary from 1841 until his death in 1871. Travis was also a naturalist and taxidermist and an itemised taxidermy bill listed some of the birds he had mounted from the aviary including teal, red mallard, gold crests, crossbill, nightjar, nuthatch, redwing and gold and silver pheasants. In 1835-6 there had been a crossbill invasion, and 8-10 years earlier in March, a pair had made a nest at Audley End aviary, in which the female deposited five eggs, but although undisturbed, deserted them without attempting incubation.[23]

The aviary was discontinued in 1885 and for the next 68 years was occupied by woodsmen and their families. The aviary became known as Ring Cottage and stood empty until 1961 when an American lady, Betty Hanley, came upon the run down building while strolling around Ring Hill. She fell in love with it and the owner, the Rt Hon Robert Neville, allowed her to rent it as a weekend country retreat for a peppercorn rent of £20 per year on a ninety-nine year lease. Betty became involved with the

Friends of Audley End and entertained at Ring Cottage until 1993 when she moved into Audley End Village. Dudley Poplak, a well-known London interior decorator, took on the tenancy of the cottage.[24]

Other Essex Aviaries

Aviaries were a popular feature in public parks during the nineteenth and twentieth centuries but the cost of their upkeep meant that most of these have been lost. Both Southchurch Park and Valentines Park had substantial aviaries. A *Historic Survey and Restoration Management Plan of Valentines Park* (1999 by Land Use Consultants), recorded the aviary in Valentines Park as still in use and sited adjacent to the Parterre Garden. This was a galvanised cage construction with a number of exotic species inside which were very popular with the public.

Many prominent Essex houses kept aviaries: Edmund Rochford owned Holmehurst, Loughton, from 1907 to 1919 and made significant changes to the garden. He built a large orchard, experimental greenhouses, a boat house on the lake and a small aviary near the enclosed orchard. Both the boathouse and the aviary were lost in the 1980s.[25] In the sales particulars for St Osyth Priory in 1983/84 in the section on outbuildings and farm buildings, mention is made of an aviary and a stone and tiled range presently used for wintering peacocks.[26] Peacocks were also kept in a wire-meshed corner of the Topiary Garden at St.Osyth. Moyns Park boasted ornate sentry like aviaries possibly of twentieth century date, which stood, and I believe still stand, either side of one of the entrances.

Old Thorndon Hall Menagerie

In 1713 Robert, seventh Lord Petre, died of smallpox at the age of twenty-four leaving his unborn son, also Robert, to be brought up by his widow. The eighth Lord Petre's grandmother had a keen interest in horticulture and her enthusiasm inspired her grandson. By 1729 Robert, then sixteen, had taken over the management of his grandmother's gardens at Thorndon and after his marriage moved to Thorndon Hall.

The 8th Lord Petre was immensely enthusiastic about botany and horticulture and in 1733 Sieur Bourgignon, a French surveyor, was employed to draw up landscape proposals and Giacomo Leoni, a Venetian architect, was commissioned to redesign the Hall. In the proposals, the stream that ran through High Wood was to be turned into a series of ponds, stretching northwards to roughly just where New Hall Pond is today. The second pond above the lake was to be the centre of the menagerie. Work on the landscape and Hall began in 1734 but was never fully completed.

One of the main features created on the 'Bourgignon Plan' was the Menagerie to house collections of animals and ornamental fowl. It was here that the 8th Lord Petre kept his exotic animals including ornamental ducks and pheasants, deer, sheep, red fowl from New England, terrapin, bustards and squirrels. These were either let loose in the park and adjoining woods or else kept in the menagerie to which Lord Petre makes reference in his correspondence more than once. A list of the servants at

Thorndon Hall in 1742 includes a Dutch 'Pheasandre' who, besides having charge of the rearing of pheasants for game purposes, almost certainly was responsible for the menagerie and the various birds such as bustards, ornamental ducks, pheasants, etc., which Lord Petre had imported from abroad and was trying to naturalise on the ponds and in the woods at Thorndon. On the 25th June 1742 Lord Petre wrote a letter to his great friend and fellow naturalist, the Quaker cloth-merchant Peter Collinson (1694-1768). He excused himself for not having visited Collinson, but he had a very bad cold, made worse by going out the previous evening. The letter ends with directions for the despatch to Thorndon of some Olive Birds which he has acquired and which were to be placed in the menagerie. On 30th June he made his will and on 2nd July he died, a victim of smallpox. He had just attained his twenty-ninth birthday.[27]

The menagerie was still in use after the death of the 8th Lord Petre as the weekly estate account books for 1788-1792 (ERO D/DP/A59) show. Several entries were made for payment for work carried out trenching by the menagerie. At the beginning of January 1788, 14s.2d. was paid for digging out 17 rods of ditch at the menagerie and another £1.9s.2d. for digging out 35 rods of the same ditch. In February 4s was paid for 12 loads of gravel for the menagerie.[28]

A County Parks Archaeological Survey of Thorndon Hall in 1994 stated that: from documentary evidence the Menagerie appears to have comprised an enclosure of c.180m square which contained animal sheds and stables in the north east corner and a central pond with an island. Earthworks in the northern part of Menagerie Plantation are believed to be traces of the rectangular enclosure used to house the animals of the Menagerie. These earthworks comprise a slight ditch and bank forming the right-angle of the north-west corner, the dammed and landscaped pond in the centre of the enclosure and traces of dam across the stream on the southern side.[29]

There can be no doubt that this menagerie was the second pond on the easterly stream above the lake, as shown on the Bourginion plan, a pond in a hollow with an island in the middle, with terraced sides, and buildings on the north-east, the whole being surrounded by a wall or palisade. It is similarly shown on Chapman and Andre's map of Essex drawn 1772-74 and on the 1778 Spyres plan, and the remains today are not difficult to identify. It has given its name to the present Menagerie Plantation.[30]

Following a survey of the menagerie plantation by Rob Adams of the Essex Gardens Trust Research Group, four horse chestnut trees in the menagerie plantation provided a range of girth measurements, the central tree measured 430cm, and the Forestry Commission's tree dating calculation places this tree at 317yrs old, with a planting date of 1692. Taking this age and dates as accurate, this would allow the suggestion that it was selected as a shade tree in Lord Petre's Menagerie, and would have been 35-40yrs old when planted, positioned centrally, and close to animal structures. Some of the hornbeams in Menagerie Plantation may also be of Lord Petre's planting .

Easton Lodge and Other Essex Menageries

Frances 'Daisy' Maynard inherited the estate of Easton Lodge in 1865 following the deaths of her father and grandfather. Daisy, the Countess of Warwick, was one of the great hostesses of the day and her weekend house parties were legendary. In 1901 the Countess commissioned Harold Peto (1854-1933) to create gardens at Easton Lodge in the Italian, French and Japanese styles.[31] By 1937 the Countess of Warwick had decided to establish a country nature reserve. The Countess had aviaries built to house her increasing number of bird species which numbered 330 at the time of her death.[32] Her interest in birds was highlighted in 1923 when, following the death of W.H. Hudson, a news cutting reported that the Countess had dedicated the wood that surrounds Stone Hall as a sanctuary for birds in memory of W.H. Hudson.[33] In addition to the aviaries the Countess had fenced off and padlocked the 4 acres surrounding Stone Hall as it was the ideal area for a large variety of birds. The park already contained birdlife which included jackdaws, green woodpeckers, goldcrests, crossbills, gold finches, long tailed tits, wood pigeons and tawny owls.[34]

Eric Hardy visited Easton Lodge in 1937 to discuss with the Countess the establishment of a county nature reserve at Easton Park after her death. The park then held some 200 red and fallow deer and about 900 St Kilda sheep and a number of Shetland ponies. Red squirrels, foxes and badgers frequented the woods around the wild duck pond. The Countess's knowledge of animals was slight and her knowledge of wildlife was virtually nil. Eric Hardy's first concern on arrival was the state of the aviaries. These she had built on the design of the 'flying school' where caged birds from the city could be released to fly in exercise before liberation. One huge cage, some twenty-two feet high completely enclosed a yew tree. Others, full of doves and budgerigars, were in a sorry state of inbred disease. The birds had never been separated and consequently they bred freely all year. The Countess was quick to appreciate her shortcomings and she promptly appointed a retired keeper from the London Zoological Gardens to regulate this side of her welfare work .

In *The Countess of Warwick*, Margaret Blunden recorded that 'as Lady Warwick grew older her devotion to the menagerie of animals that surrounded her strengthened its hold, and she lost none of her strange benign power over wild life. Visitors to the park might catch a glimpse of Lady Warwick standing alone, with rare birds perched without fear on her outstretched arms and picture hat'.[35]

Frances, Countess of Warwick, died on 26th July 1938 aged 77. She left an annuity to her housekeeper, Nancy Galpin, along with trunks full of clothes worn in her glittering heyday as hostess, as well as her pet dogs and birds. The birds were an embarrassing legacy for the housekeeper as there were no fewer than five hundred of them. The housekeeper said that the Countess did not know that it cost £8 per week to feed them and sent more than two hundred budgerigars and canaries to the RSPCA in East Molesey, Surrey. The housekeeper moved to a little house on the estate where there was room for only a small aviary, taking just one hundred birds with her, the ones her ladyship loved most.[36] On the morning of 26th July, the day of the Countess' death, a telegram had arrived at the Lodge to say that one hundred head of highland cattle, ordered by Lady Warwick for the park, were on their way by rail from Scotland. Maynard, her long suffering heir, desperately telegrammed station after station along the line to get the cattle turned back. His mother was dead.'[37] All her life the Countess had been devoted to horses and it is appropriate that one of the last photographs of Daisy, shortly before her death, should be with the retired circus ponies to whom she gave a last home at the Lodge.[38] During the war the parkland the Countess had pictured as a sanctuary for bird life became an airfield; the old trees were uprooted as concrete runways were laid and animals and rare birds scattered in confusion.[39] Most of the monkeys she had doted on were shot.

In a *Scheme for a Menagerie* for Copped Hall (1747), John Conyers and Sir Roger Newdigate produced sketches for the layout of grounds of new Copped Hall including a plan for the menagerie and an extensive building for fowls in the stable area. However, it seems that John Conyers did not have sufficient funds to carry out his plans and the menagerie was never built.[40] Another Essex menagerie of which there is little information was kept at Rivenhall Place by Mrs Steele, a novelist, who lived there during the nineteenth century. The estate map (ERO D/DQy/22) of Debden Hall shows the layout of gardens, park and menagerie in relation to the house and gives a very detailed plan of the layout of the menagerie, but unfortunately there are no references to the animals and birds kept there.[41]

Wombwell and the Travelling Menageries

George Wombwell (1777-1850), proprieter of one of the most famous of the travelling menageries, was born in Essex and as a boy devoted much of his time to the breeding and rearing of birds, pigeons, rabbits and dogs. He was by trade a cordwainer in Soho's Old Compton Street, but his life changed when he saw some of the first boa constrictors to be imported into England. He bought a pair, reputedly for £75, and soon recovered this expenditure by exhibiting them at great fairs throughout the Country. His menagerie was conveyed in brightly painted wagons in market squares in provincial towns. The animals exhibited in the early years included elephants, lions, tigers, leopards, panthers, hyenas, zebras, camels, jackals, apes, baboons and monkeys. Among birds were a golden eagle, emus, cockatoos, and parakeets. Later a rhinoceros was added, with giraffes, a puma, a polar bear, black and brown bears, porcupines, a Brahman cow, and many more. As the number of animals in the menagerie grew, Wombwell split his show firstly into two, and then into three, separate menageries. By 1843 there were sixteen wagons in the first of his shows, which remained popular despite, or perhaps because of, numerous accidents to members of the public and the death of Wombwell's niece, Ellen Blight the 'Lion Queen', when an enraged tiger attacked and killed her in full view of spectators.[42]

The travelling menageries were later known as Bostock and Wombwell's menageries. In the St James's Church of England School, Halstead, log book mention is made on the 15th December 1905 that a half day holiday was given to visit the Bostock and Wombwell's menagerie at Halstead. The mistress took thirty of the children to hear a lecture on the animals, and to witness the performances of the various animals there. An earlier entry mentions another half day holiday when children were taken to see a wild beast show and circus at Halstead on 3rd May 1897.[43]

Conclusion

References to historic Essex menageries and aviaries are scarce despite the popularity of both during the eighteenth century. Menageries were often placed at the edge of the park, as in the case of Debden Hall, where they were surrounded by trees or woodland or, as at Thorndon Hall, were associated with a lake. By the end of the nineteenth century the private menagerie was fast disappearing from country estates, through a fall in popularity and by the cost of the upkeep of the animals. Very few private menageries exist today, and although some of their buildings remain they can be difficult to identify. The story is the same for aviaries, although they survived longer than the menageries. It was easier to keep an aviary, they could be small indoor ones, usually kept in a conservatory or ornamental outdoor cages as seen at Moyns Park. Exotic animals and birds can still be seen in Essex but not usually as part of the large private estate. Several Essex farms have opened to the public housing many types of animals and birds: these are no longer just for pleasure but are also for profit as their popularity shows. Today the Menagerie Plantation forms part of Thorndon Country Park and is managed by the Essex County Council. Menagerie Plantation is a Site of Special Scientific Interest.

Bibliography

Published Sources

Blunden, M., 1967 *The Countess of Warwick,* Cassell

Buttery, D., 1988 *Portraits of a Lady,* Brewin Books

Clutton, Sir G. & Mackay, C., 1970 'Old Thorndon Hall, Essex: a History and Reconstruction of its Park and Garden' in *Garden History Occasional Papers,* 2, 27-39

Essex Gardens Trust, 2004 Epping Forest District: Inventory of Designed Landscapes (unpublished MS)

Festing, S., 1988 'Menageries and the landscape garden' in *Journal of Garden History,* 8, iv, 104-117

Green, N. & Cooper, J. 2001 The American Bittern – an historic first for Essex in *Saffron Walden Historical Journal No 1*

Hadfield, M., 1960 *A History of British Gardening,* Hamlyn

Hardy, E., 1968 'Memories of an Essex Animal Lover', in *Essex Countryside* November 1968, **17**, No 142, 36-37

Hibberd, S., 1867 *Rustic Adornments for Homes of Taste,* ('Aviaries' pgs 201-216) Reprint Century Hutchinson/National Trust (1987)

Hunt, P., (ed) 1964 *Shell Gardens Book*, Rainbird Ltd

King, R., 1974 *The Quest for Paradise,* Mayflower Books, New York

Lang, T., 1966 *My Darling Daisy,* Michael Joseph

Magnus, I., & Spencer-Jones, R., 2000 *The History of Easton Lodge:* (On behalf of Easton Lodge)

McCann, T.J., 1994 'Much troubled with very rude company...,' in *Sussex Archaeological Collections,* 132, 143-149

Saunders, L., & Williamson, G., (eds) 2005 *Littlebury, A Parish History,* The History Group of the Parish of Littlebury Millennium Society

Sutherill, M., 1995 The Gardens of Audley End English Heritage

Sutherill, M., 1997 'Creature Comforts, the Rise and Fall of the Menagerie' in *Essex Gardens Trust Newsletter* Autumn 1997

Thacker, C., 1979 *The History of Gardens,* Croom Helm

Wilkinson, E. & Henderson, M., (eds.) 1992 *The Garden Ornament Sourcebook,* Cassell

Primary Sources

1747 Scheme for a Menagerie ERO D/DW/E28/5

1783 Estate Map of Saffron Walden and Littlebury ERO D/DQy8

1788-1792 Weekly Estate account book for Thorndon (ERO D/DP/A59)

1840 Estate map of Debden menagerie ERO D/DQy/22

1894-1909 St.James's Church of England School, Greenstead Green, Halstead Log Book (ERO E/ML 127/4)

1983/4 St Osyth's Priory Sales document Sole agents: Knight Frank & Rutley

Undated and unnamed newscutting in the Easton Lodge archives.

Websites

www.news.bbc.co.uk *Big cats prowled London's tower*

www.follies.org.uk *The Menagerie in Europe: an overview* and *The Menagerie at home* Issue 15 July 2008

www.oxforddnb.com *George Wombwell* by George Speaight

www.unlockingessex.essexcc.gov.uk *County Parks Archaeological Survey – Thorndon Park* 1994 SMR Number 19613

www.gardenhistorysociety.org/post/agenda/the-new-elizabethan-garden-at-Kenilworth-Castle

www.recordinguttlesfordhistory/org.uk/saffronwalden/americanbittern

References

1   Saunders & Williams 2005, 120
2   Wilkinson & Henderson 1992, 14-15
3   Thacker 1979, 19-20
4   King 1974, 84
5   Wilkinson & Henderson 1992, 14-15
6   King, 1974, 88-89
7   www.gardenhistorysociety.org/post/agenda/the-new-elizabethan-garden-at-Kenilworth-Castle
8   Hadfield 1960, 165
9   Wilkinson & Henderson 1992, 14-15
10 Hunt, 1964, 93
11 www.news.bbc.co.uk
12 www.follies.org.uk The Menagerie in Europe: an overview Issue 15 July 2008
13 Hunt 1964, 154
14 www.follies.org.uk The Menagerie in Europe: an overview Issue 15 July 2008
15 Festing 1988, 104-117
16 McCann 1994
17 www.follies.org.uk The Menagerie at home Issue 15 July 2008
18 Sutherill 1997
19 The hillfort on the hill was apparently known as 'Starberry' in the medieval period.
20 Saunders & Williamson 2005, 118-120
21 Saunders & Williamson 2005, 118-120
22 Saunders & Williamson 2005, 118-120
23 www.recordinguttlesfordhistory/org.uk/saffronwalden/americanbittern
24 Saunders & Williamson 2005, 118-120
25 Essex Gardens Trust 2004
26 St Osyth's Priory Sales document 1983/4 Sole agents: Knight Frank & Rutley
27 Clutton & Mackay 1970
28 Weekly Estate account book for Thorndon 1788-92 ERO D/DP/A59
29 www.unlockingessex.essexcc.gov.uk County Parks Archaeological Survey – Thorndon Park 1994 SMR Number 19613
30 Clutton & Mackay 1970
31 Magnus & Spencer-Jones 2000 5,11,16
32 Magnus & Spencer-Jones 2000 26
33 Easton Lodge archives
34 Hardy1968
35 Blunden 1967, 322
36 Lang 1967, 190-1
37 Blunden 1967, 327
38 Buttery 1988, 42 & 47
39 Blunden 1967, 327
40 Scheme for a Menagerie 1747, ERO D/DW/E28/5
41 Estate map of Debden menagerie 1840 ERO D/DQy/22
42 www.oxforddnb.com George Wombwell by George Speaight
43 St.James's Church of England School, Greenstead Green, Halstead Log Book 1894-1909 ERO E/ML 127/4

The Essex Stable: functional building or status symbol?

by Penelope Keys

Willowcote, 94 Main Road, Danbury, Essex CM3 4DH

Introduction

The horse played a central role in British society until it was superseded by the motor car following the First World War. Horses used for work or display had to be housed if they were to perform at their best and be kept secure. However, the stables of large country houses became more than just a warm, safe environment in which to keep horses: they became a status symbol, like the horses themselves. The position of the stables in relation to the houses and their architectural styling reflected the changing fashions of the day. It is this relationship between the stable and the house in Essex which will be the main focus of this study. Aspects which will be considered include: distance between the stable block and the house, direction from the house, was it attached to the house or apart, visual impact from the house, status of the building in terms of architectural style and materials?

Background History of Stables in Britain

Remains of stables have been found dating back to the Roman period. Noteworthy Roman examples having been found at Brough-on-Noe in Derbyshire and Ilkley in Yorkshire. There is little evidence for the Saxon period, but some medieval stables are better documented and a few are still extant, including the Archbishop's Stables in Maidstone, Kent, which date from the early fourteenth century.[1]

The country house stable came to prominence as a distinct building type in the late sixteenth and early seventeenth centuries. The reign of Elizabeth I saw a new interest in architecture and as great houses were altered and rebuilt, so were their stables. Previously stables had been positioned with other service buildings in an outer court, but they were now isolated from these and given greater prominence in the landscape. They were now clearly visible in the approach to the house. The first book to be published in this period with advice on stable construction was Thomas Blundeville's *The Fower Chiefyst Offices Belonging to Horsemanshippe* (1565). Blundeville recommended that stables should be positioned so that the owner 'may have a delight to come always thither to see his horse. For according to the olde proverb that the horse is most commonlie fat which is fedde with his own masters eye'.[2] Royal stables of this period started to be built as quadrangles, for example at Hampton Court (1537-38). During the late-sixteenth to early seventeenth centuries, the 'traditional' half timbered stables with brick bases began to fall out of

favour and new stables were increasingly constructed entirely of stone or brick with slate or tile roofs (replacing thatch) and glazed windows. The stables of Old Thorndon Hall in Essex, for example, were tiled as early as 1589. The early seventeenth century stables at Blickling Hall in Norfolk were constructed as symmetrical wings on either side of a forecourt, giving them even greater prominence in relation to the house. In the Stuart period a few new stable ranges were built as quadrangles, early examples were Petworth in Sussex (built between 1616 and 1623 and now destroyed) and Theobolds in Hertfordshire (constructed 1607-1610). This formation was to become common in the eighteenth century having previously been reserved for Royal stables.

The stables at Audley End (Essex) whose construction is thought to have started in 1603, were not visible from the main approach to the house and their style of construction is old-fashioned compared to that of the great house itself. This is in part due to the functional needs of stables and was common to many examples. Elizabethan and Jacobean houses were increasingly constructed with large windows and flat roofs, neither of which would be suitable for a stable. Stables needed much less light inside and their pitched roofs allowed space for grooms sleeping quarters and haylofts. One notable introduction in the Stuart stable was the *oeil de boeuf* window. This classical detail allowed lighting and ventilation into haylofts. They were usually set above casement windows which illuminated the stables proper. This was also the period when cupola was introduced. They were originally used on houses, but remained popular as a feature of stable architecture for far longer. In the house the cupola formed a viewing platform, but in the stable it often housed a bell and clock. It was most usually centrally positioned on the stable block and made into a conspicuous feature.

As the seventeenth century progressed other buildings joined the stable range: riding houses (for the exercise of horses indoors), separate rooms for grooms and tack, and coach houses. Coaches had become common by the end of the sixteenth century and the need to house these and the larger horses needed to pull them, brought about more improvements in stable design.

In the second half of the seventeenth century stables began to be incorporated into one of the wings of the house itself, echoing the formation of the Jacobean stables at Blickling Hall. Stanstead Park in Surrey was built in this style.

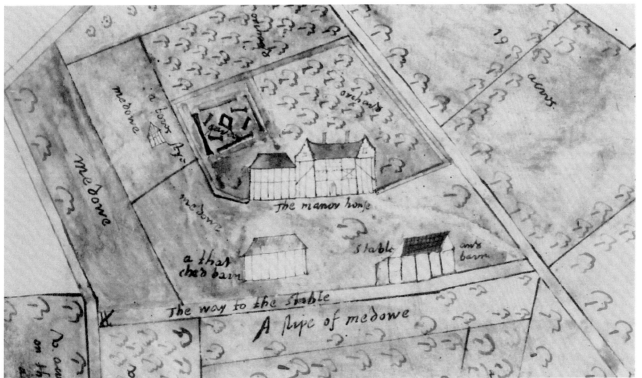

Figure 1 *Estate map of Purleigh Hall (c.1600). (ERO D/DGE P1) (Reproduced by courtesy of the Essex Record Office.)*

The move to Palladian architecture in the eighteenth century saw the stable block become a detached quadrangle, placed to one side of the house. A few builders still favoured wings, but most landowners felt that the quadrangle, once a royal prerogative, made a greater statement about their power and position in society. Today the abiding image of a Georgian stable is the quadrangle with the cupola rising above it. The detached quadrangle had various advantages: it moved the smell of horses away from the house and its single entrance provided security for these valuable animals. Robert Morris, in his *Lectures on Architecture* suggested that the ideal villa should have gardens on three sides with a kitchen garden on the final side, slightly removed and the stables beyond that 'remote from the house'.[3] At this time even modest country houses, such as Dynes Hall in Essex, boasted their own fashionable stable blocks.

In the late Georgian period stable design underwent another revolution, similar to that initiated by the introduction of the coach horse. The catalyst in this case was the thoroughbred: a horse bred specifically for racing and hunting. To accommodate these fine horses the old stalls were replaced by loose boxes, each at least 10ft square. Concern to improve the conditions in which horses were kept also led to improvements in ventilation and drainage. These improvements can still be seen at the Exeter House stables in Newmarket, which were built 1820.

The Victorian era saw interest in stable building reach its peak. Almost fifty books appeared which included at least one chapter on stable construction; ten were published in the 1860s alone. Drainage and ventilation continued to be major concerns. The garden and landscape writer J.C. Loudon (1783-1843) advocated 'large, cool, well ventilated, south-east facing stables'.[4] Large windows were favoured and ventilation tubes, which took stale air

out through the roof. Brick floors incorporated drainage channels and could be easily cleaned. There was great debate over the issue of open or closed drains, but whichever was favoured it was recognised that horses should not stand in a wet environment. Great attention was given to the interior decoration of the stables, with colour themed tiling and catalogues such as Millers offering matching manger and hay-rack sets.[5] In some stables gas lighting was introduced, this being considered to be the safest option. Running water was also brought into every stall. A few stables even had central heating, including those at Avery Hill in Greenwich (1885-91). Tack rooms and grooms quarters were also enlarged and improved.

New stables were built during this period in a range of architectural styles, from Gothic to Elizabethan, with a move away from Georgian symmetry to the more broken and romantic outline favoured by the Picturesque movement. This trend saw stables move closer to the main house again. Georgian stables, however, had been solidly and generously built and many continued to be used, refitted inside with all the latest Victorian innovations. Some landowners still favoured the quadrangular form, as can be seen in the new stables built at Wimpole Hall, Cambridgeshire, during this period.

By the last decade of the nineteenth century it was felt that little more could be done to improve stables. In 1907, Professor J. Wortley Axe declared in his work *The Horse, Its Treatment in Health and Disease III*, 'In no other country so much as Britain is the horse at once the friend and companion of man, and in no other country is it so well housed'.[6] The turn of the century saw some large stables being built. A particularly attractive example being the elegant quadrangle built in the Adamesque style at Manderston House in Berkshire. The construction of these stables began in 1895. In 1901 the main house was remodelled and the new structures included a range of garages. With the growth in use of the motor car for transport, so the use of the horse declined. Coach houses were converted into garages and although horses were retained for hunting, there was little justification for the construction of new stables. The golden era of stable building was over.

The Development of Stables in Essex

This study has been principally based on the evidence provided by maps housed in the Essex Record Office, with supplementary evidence from written sources where this is available. For each of the estates researched the date, architectural style, and location of the stables (in relation to the house and the entrance to the estate) was established where possible. Over thirty estates were examined, although not all are discussed here.

The study commences in the sixteenth century. Evidence for this period is supplied by the beautifully illustrated Walker maps. One of the earliest of these is the 1598 map of Thorndon Hall. Here the stables are situated to the east of the house. They form a large three-sided structure clearly visible from the front of the house and appear to be of very high status. These stables were later destroyed and rebuilt with the new Thorndon Hall in the late eighteenth century.

From a similar date (1600) is an estate map of Purleigh Hall (*Figure 1*). This is a modest timber-framed building, in no way similar to the prominent Elizabethan house that was Thorndon Hall, but still we see the stables to the front of the house and clearly marked, suggesting that their owner felt that their presence there increased his status.

Rivenhall Place was originally a Tudor building,[7] and it is possible that the stables seen to the southeast of the house in the 1716 estate map were of a similar date to the house. Once again the stables are visible from the front of the house, which faces south-southeast. Architecturally they appear to have been a utilitarian structure and part of a complex of buildings including a barn (*Figure 2*). Like Thorndon, these stables were rebuilt elsewhere on the site in the eighteenth century.

The 1611 Walker map of Old and New Peverels, in the Hundred of Chelmsford (both no longer in existence) shows Old Peverels as a modest building with what appears to be a stable block in front of it; New Peverels, however, is a much grander house with an Elizabethan appearance and this seems to have its stable block behind the house (*Figure 3*). Cartographic evidence suggests most Essex landowners of the sixteenth century saw their stables as an enhancement to their property and consequently built them in full view of their the front of their houses. New Peverels however seems to be an exception.

Belhus, near Aveley, in South Essex dates to the later sixteenth century. The Royal Commission for Historical Monuments (RCHM) described the earliest of Belhus' stables as follows:

> 'The *Stable* ..., to the SE of the house, is a rectangular building of two storeys with attics. The walls are brick; the roofs are tiled. It was built in the late sixteenth century with N and S gabled walls...'[8]

This would seem to have been another high status building. It appears to have been close to the house. The stables later had a 'modern' extension (RCHM) .

Probably the best known extant stable block in Essex is that at Audley End. Although at a short distance from the house, this block was a high status building, intended

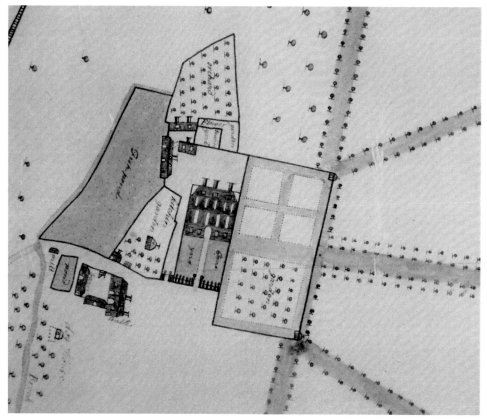

Figure 2. Estate map of Rivenhall Place (1716). (ERO D/DFg P1/18). (Reproduced by courtesy of the Essex Record Office.)

Figure 3 New Peverels House (1611). (ERO D/DZT 5) (Reproduced by courtesy of the Essex Record Office.)

to be shown to interested visitors. The RCHM gives a lengthy description of this building:

> The stables, NNW of the house,... are of three stories, the walls are of brick, and the roofs are tiled. They...

form one long range with a slightly projecting cross-wing in the middle and at each end. On the *N Elevation* ... the storeys are divided by plain brick bands and the three wings are gabled; in the middle wing is a wide round-headed archway flanked by pilasters which support a pediment with blind tracery of Gothic character. Between the wings are semi-octagonal bay windows with rounded lights and transoms ... The *S Elevation* is similar to the N elvation, but between the wings are three gabled dormers and there are no bay windows...[9]

At Langleys in Great Waltham the early seventeenth century stables were northeast of the house. They have 'walls of red brick and the roofs are tiled. The stable has two original gabled dormers ...' [10] On the Chapman and Andre map of 1777 the stables look to be a little removed from the house (*Figure 5*).

Another early seventeenth century stable block which attracted the attention of the RCHM was at Albyns at Stapleford Abbots. Like Belhus this was another large house and estate. The Royal Commission date this stable to approximately 1620. It was another brick and tile construction, two storeys high. They comment that the 'original gables have moulded copings and brick finials; the original windows have moulded and plastered jambs and mullions.'[11] They were situated to the east of the house. There is an image of Albyns on the Chapman and Andre maps, but it is not possible to tell from this which of the buildings to the east of the house is the stables, however most of these would have been visible from the main approach.[12] These stables were also subject to eighteenth century improvements.

The final seventeenth century stable blocks in the current research were at Waltons, near Ashdon. These were south of the house and 'consist of two rectangular blocks, each of two storeys; the walls are of brick and the

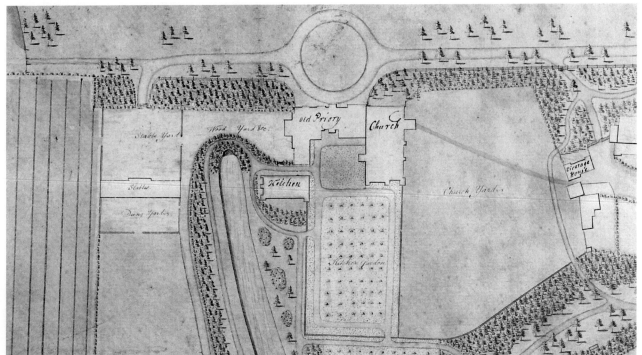

Figure 4 Recommendations for improvements to Hatfield Priory (1765). (ERO D/DBR P2) (Reproduced with kind permission of the Essex Record Office.)

Figure 5 Langleys: Chapman and Andre (1777) (D/DBy P9). (Reproduced by courtesy of the Essex Record Office.)

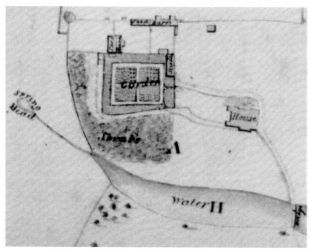

Figure 6 Estate map of Rivenhall Place (1825) (ERO D/DFg P9). (Reproduced by courtesy of the Essex Record Office.)

roofs are tiled. Both blocks were built in the early seventeenth century.'[13] The RCHM describe both blocks as having mullioned windows and the north block as having an interesting central chimney stack consisting of four shafts in a star shaped plan.

As discussed earlier, new stables built in the seventeenth century were often attached to the house in the form of a forecourt. The stables at Waltons are the only ones which I have found where there would seem to have been two facing stable blocks, however the RCHM make no mention of them being attached to the house.

In the eighteenth century there was a great flurry of rebuilding and alteration of stables in Essex. One of the innovations of this period was the coach house; in some cases these were added to existing stables, as at Albyns. At Braxted Park, near Witham, however, a new stable complex was built and attached to the house which included a 'two-storey arched, pedimented gateway, and pedimented three-bay coachhouse on the east side with domed bellcote'.[14] Some stables were simply updated so that they appeared to fit the fashions of the day. This was the case at Copford Hall. During the eighteenth century the Hall was subject to rebuilding and alteration and its original timber-framed stables were given a classical make-over with the addition of a white brick front with red brick dressings.[15]

The eighteenth century saw a fashion for stables in the quadrangular form, embellished with clock towers and cupolas. The latter two features appeared on the stables at Dynes Hall in Great Maplestead by 1770, but without the classical quadrangle. Shortgrove Hall near Newport in the northwest corner of Essex also had an impressive stable block which Pevsner describes as follows: 'Two storeys, with clock tower and open cupola topped with a dome over the central archway... Eleven bays, the outer bays and the central, pedimented bay stepping slightly forward.'[16]

The stables at Shortgrove were still visible from the main approach to the house, but the trend in the eighteenth century was to move new stable blocks further away from the house.

The landscape designer Humphry Repton was

especially concerned that such buildings would not detract from his designs and should be removed from sight or given an attractive facade. Rivenhall Place was Repton's first commission in Essex, undertaken in 1789. Here he was not happy with the stables, which, as we have already seen were a prominent feature in front and to the southeast of the house *(Figure 2)*. An estate map of 1825 shows them rebuilt well away behind the house and to the north-northeast *(see Figure 6)*. Hylands House near Chelmsford was another site which benefited from Repton's input. He appears to have visited the house sometime after 1797,[17] and it would seem to have been as a result of his suggestions that the new stable court was built at the back of the house, this included '3 coach houses and a chaise house; harness and saddle rooms'.[18] This impressive structure is still extant.

Another site where improvements were suggested to shield the stables from the house was Hatfield Priory *(Figure 4)*. There is no firm evidence to suggest that the stables were reconstructed in this way and they appear to have remained adjacent to the canal until their removal in the 1970s.[19]

One of the grandest new houses in Essex constructed in the eighteenth century was Wanstead. Wanstead was rebuilt between 1715 and 1722,[20] becoming one of the greatest Palladian mansions of the age. An engraving of 1715 shows what appears to be a large stable block close to the south side of the house; after the improvements the stables were rebuilt to the north of the house and much further away *(Figure 7)*.

This 1813 map shows the stables within clear view of the house, but a map of 1825 shows them screened by trees *(Figure 8)*. One aspect of this rebuilding which may appear odd, is that the new stable block was built very close to the church. By 1973 'the 18th-century stable court, of brick and weather-boarded timber', survived as a golf club house.[21] The main house was sold for demolition in 1823, but what is interesting is not that the stables survive (this is quite common where the main house has been destroyed the stables are often converted into a dwelling, being of a more normal house size by modern standards than the original house) but that they were

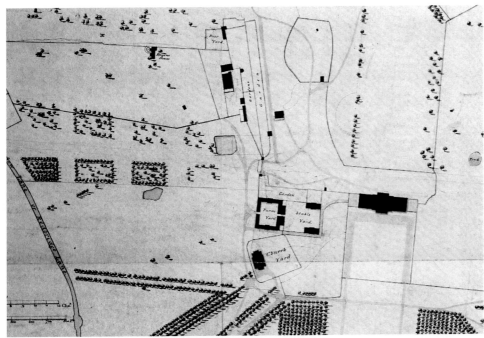

Figure 7 *Estate map of Wanstead House (1813). (ERO D/DCW P20) (Reproduced by courtesy of the Essex Record Office.)*

made of such modest materials. This is the age of the grand quadrangular stable blocks and the new Wanstead House was a very prestigious building and much admired, 'even Horace Walpole, who was inclined to ridicule the taste of its parvenu owners, admitted to the grandeur of the scene.'[22] It is therefore rather strange that the stables were built of brick and weather-boarded, perhaps this is why the trees were planted, as a visual shield.

Humphrey Repton continued his commissions in Essex in the nineteenth century. In 1808 he made recommendations for Moor Hall, near Harlow.[23] Here he suggested that the stable block either be moved further away from the house and out of sight, or that it should be made more attractive with the addition of an ornamental facade: it seems likely that the second option was followed. The surviving stable block does have the classical, and indeed, grand appearance which we associate with such buildings at this period. The clock tower and cupola on this

building has become a very solid structure. In 1813 Repton also put his stamp on the grounds of Woodford Hall. Here the stables were already some little distance away to the north of the house and screened by mature trees. He appears to have been content with this and merely suggested removing the poultry yard to the south-east of the stables.[24]

In the nineteenth century, several Essex stable blocks were remodelled to suit the fashions of the day. As discussed above, these fashions were various, ranging from Gothic to Elizabethan, but all providing a more broken outline than was favoured in the Georgian period. Wivenhoe Park was one such case. The original house was built in 1759, but 'it was enlarged and remodelled in neo-Tudor style for J. G. Rebow in 1846-53 ... The main additions were to the east where he added service rooms which adjoined a new stable yard which is dated 1846.'[25] It is interesting to note that in a map from 1765 entitled

Figure 8 *Estate map of Wanstead House (c.1825) (ERO D/DCW P61). (Reproduced by courtesy of the Essex Record Office.)*

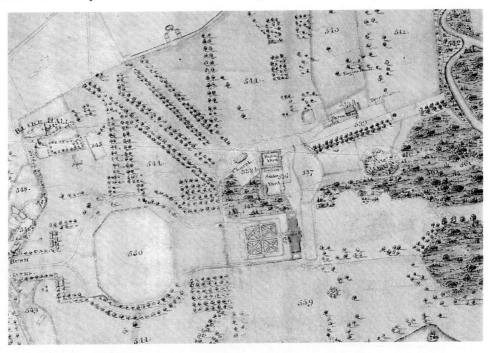

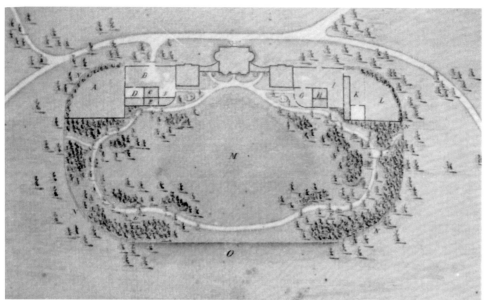

Figure 9
Recommendations for the improvement of Wivenhoe Park (1765). (ERO T/M 271) (Reproduced by courtesy of the Essex Record Office.)

'Design for the improvement of Wivenhoe Park ...' the stable yard (marked 'B' on the map) is to the west (*Figure 9*). Pevsner records that the west wing disappeared in the remodelling.[26]

Faulkbourne Hall, itself an impressive fifteenth century structure, was also given mock Tudor stables in the nineteenth century, complete with a clock dated 1844. The previous stables had been to the south of the house, the replacements were to the east. Another site where remodelling took place was Copped Hall, near Epping Upland. In 1895-6 Charles Eamer Kempe redesigned the garden in 'Renaissance' style and at this point Pevsner records that the stables were remodelled with the addition of a 'lead-covered clock tower and bell-cote'.[27]

Stables in the Twentieth Century

What has become of these interesting structures in the twentieth century? Some disappeared long ago, but others have found new uses. Where the large house has gone, as at Shortgrove and Markshall (near Coggeshall) the stables themselves have sometimes been converted into dwellings (*Figure 10*).

At Braxted Park the house is still extant and the site is now used as a wedding and conference venue. Where the houses are open to the public, large classically styled stable blocks and their associated buildings seem to suggest themselves as suitable for conversion to restaurants and shops, as has happened at Wimpole Hall (Cambridgeshire), Chatsworth (Derbyshire), Renishaw Hall (Derbyshire), and in Essex at Hylands House, near Chelmsford.

Conclusions

Over thirty estates were examined and the following aspects considered: distance between the stable block and the house, direction from the house, was it attached to the house or apart, visual impact from the house, status of the building in terms of architectural style and materials. The following conclusions were reached based on this sample:

The distance of the stable block from the house, whether or not it was attached and whether it was intended to be seen by visitors to the property appears to have been directly connected with the status of the stable building. Even the earliest examples, such as old Thorndon Hall, Purleigh Hall and Old Peverels included stable buildings that were positioned close to the house and in view of its main approach, if not actually in front of it. There are exceptions, such as Audley End, where the stables were clearly a very high status building, but were not in the immediate vicinity of the house, although here the pre-eighteenth century entrance route would have meant that the stables were visible to visitors on approach.

Figure 10 Stables at Markshall. (Author's Photograph, 2009.)

Figure 11 Coach houses at Markshall. One of the coach houses is used for wedding receptions, while the roof space of the other has been converted into offices (Author's Photograph, 2009.)

The seventeenth century generally saw a move to building stable blocks as projecting wings at the front of the house, but I found no examples of this among my sample of Essex stables. The abiding image of the eighteenth century stable block is the great detached, stone built quadrangle, complete with clock tower and cupola; several fine buildings were built with the clock tower and cupola, but it is not until we come to Hylands House in the early years of the nineteenth century (I have been unable to find an exact date for the construction of the stables) that we see this quadrangle in all its glory within Essex.

Finally we come to the question of the direction of the building from the house. The only direction which was almost always avoided in my sample was west, presumably because that is the prevailing wind direction for much of inland Britain and therefore the direction that was most likely to bring the smells of the stable to the house. The most popular directions were north or east and the points in between, indeed northeast and north-northeast were some of the most favoured directions: Copford Hall and the rebuilt Rivenhall stables were both north-northeast of the house. Navestock Hall and Markshall stables were both to the northeast; those of Wanstead and Rivenhall were to the north; and the old Thorndon stables were to the east of the house and so were the stables at Braxted. Wivenhoe Park may originally have had stables as part of its west wing, but these were replaced in the mid-nineteenth century with stables to the east. The only other example that I found of stables being deliberately rebuilt to the west was the new Thorndon Hall, where they formed part of the West wing (Pevsner suggests that the stables of Hylands House are to the west, but they appear to me to actually be to the northwest of the house[28]).

The proximity of Essex to London has ensured that it has had a substantial number of grand houses, and many of these houses were constructed with fine stable blocks in close proximity to the house, presumably with the intention that they should enhance the status of their owner. We have seen that this trend appears to have also extended to smaller dwellings such Purleigh Hall, Old Peverels and Waltons, although in some cases the proximity to the house may simply have been a matter of convenience for the owner and possibly also for security. The ownership of horses was clearly a necessity for purposes of transport, but it was also a status symbol and the housing of those animals was seen in the same light. This has left us with a selection of interesting and often impressive buildings to enjoy in our own century.

Bibliography

Bettley, J. & Pevsner N 2007 *The Buildings of England: Essex,* Yale University Press

Cooper, J. (ed), 2001 *Victoria County History of Essex,* 10, Oxford University Press

Cowell, F. & Green G. (eds), 2000 *Repton in Essex,* Essex Gardens Trust

Foreman, S. 1999 *Hylands, the story of an Essex Country House and its Owners,* Redwood Books

Powell, C. 1991 *Stables and Stable Blocks,* Shire Publications

Powell, W.R. (ed), 1973 *Victoria County History of Essex,* 6, Oxford University Press

Royal Commission on Historical Monuments, 1916 *An Inventory of the Historical Monuments of Essex,* 1, HMSO

Royal Commission on Historical Monuments, 1921 *An Inventory of the Historical Monuments of Essex,* 2, HMSO

Royal Commission on Historical Monuments, 1923 *An Inventory of the Historical Monuments of Essex,* 4, HMSO

Turner, S-A., 2005 'Moor or less? An assessment of the implementation and survival of Humphry Repton's recommendations concerning Moor Hall in Harlow, Essex', in Way, T. (ed) *Paper Landscapes,* Essex Gardens Trust, 25-34

Worsley, G., 2004 *The English Stable,* Yale University Press

References

1 Powell C. 1991, 3
2 Blundeville 1565, 10, quoted in Worsley 2004
3 Morris 1734, 161, quoted in Worsley, 2004
4 Powell C. 1991, 18
5 Powell C. 1991, 23
6 Axe 1907, 319, quoted in Worsley 2004, 269
7 Bettley & Pevsner 2007, 645
8 RCHM 1923, 6
9 RCHM 1916, 238-9
10 RCHM 1921, 107
11 RCHM 1921, 225
12 Cowell & Green, 16
13 RCHM 1916, 13-14
14 Bettley & Pevsner 2007, 394
15 Cooper 2001, 144
16 Bettley & Pevsner 2007, 612
17 Cowell & Green, 81
18 Foreman 1999, 27
19 Fiona Cowell 2009, pers. comm.
20 Powell W.R.1973, 325
21 Powell W.R. 1973, 326.
22 Ibid, 326
23 Turner 2005, 25
24 Cowell & Green 2000, 183
25 Cooper 2001, 282
26 Bettley & Pevsner 2007, 800
27 ibid, 308
28 Bettley & Pevsner 2007, 501

Animals in the Landscape at Thorndon Hall, Essex

Robert Adams

c/o Writtle College, Chelmsford, Essex CM1 3RR

Introduction

During the sixteenth to nineteenth centuries there was a fascination with exotic animals among the higher echelons of English society; some were kept for their ornamental characteristics and others for possible domestication, but all were symbolic of elite family status.[1] The eighteenth century landscape design ideas popularised by Bridgeman and others, using the ha-ha to 'call in the country', allowed domesticated animals to become a part of the landscape's 'picturesque' appeal – a living landscape feature.[2] Menageries on country estates varied in construction, but were often façades or pavilions containing screened pens, frequently housing only birds, being merely semi- or non-permanent structures.[3] In addition, aviaries, game stores, kennels, stables and other animal-related buildings were common on large estates.

Thorndon Hall, Essex, one of two principal residences acquired by the Petre family in the 1570s,[4] is a large site with historical longevity and a high potential for containing archaeological evidence relating to structures associated with animals. Thorndon remained in the Petre family for four hundred years; it has a long association with animals inside its park and its manorial parish. Hatch Farm was built as a 'Model Farm' for the Thorndon Estate, specifically for the rearing of deer and cattle on the estate.[5] Thorndon was chosen for site-specific analysis because documentary evidence for this estate in Essex has been studied thoroughly by A.C. Edwards and Nancy Briggs, revealing large amounts of information accumulated over four centuries. The techniques used for investigating structures associated with animals on the Thorndon estate include literary and archival documentation, maps, aerial photography, site survey and Geographical Information System (GIS) technology. Historical archaeology theory states that, '... archaeological interpretations gain strength by moving back and forth between multiple lines of evidence, a process referred to ... as 'tracking' ... this approach allows ... multiple interpretations of the historical past.'[6] This investigation utilised such a method of interpretation to examine the animal-related structures and to draw conclusions about their construction, placement and use.

The investigation was divided into three phases: the first used regressive mapping to investigate changes in the estate layout and plotted any noted association to animals, the second examined literary and archival evidence for animals in the landscape, and the final stage used map and literary evidence to locate and interpret earthworks by cross-referencing GPS co-ordinates with co-ordinates plotted and generated using GIS.

Methodology

Regressive mapping was initiated using modern OS maps to locate the site and identify the 10km British National Grid (BNG) reference for Thorndon Park: TQ68, TQ69. These were divided into 1km BNG references for visual studies in GIS. 1km references identified the required OS 1st ed. 25" maps (1868), allowing data collection of detailed mapping to further visual analysis. This process identified a list of features for further investigation, established a time line and developed a strategy which supported the other lines of enquiry employed during this study.

Essex County Council (ECC), kindly supplied digitised estate maps, which allowed the temporal analysis to extend back to 1598, showing the key stages of landscape change and development since the estate's purchase by the Petre family in the 1570s. These estate maps were processed and re-scaled to make them compatible with modern OS mapping data using GIS.

This process required literary documentation (to interpret features), archaeological reports, maps and photographic evidence, which created site specific mapping to guide the surveying, correlated layers of data, and supplied additional data for a second survey. The second survey was necessary to identify features which could not be located accurately during the first, allowing a detailed survey to focus on just two features, rather than all the structures associated with animals. The two surveys were carried out a week apart. This allowed time for reviewing the mapping and adding the data collected from the first survey to refine the search areas. Additional survey work investigated the menagerie and old stable block to pin down their locations, while assessing their relationships with other features in the landscape. GIS allowed the generation of mapping for visual research and provided data for cross-referencing on the ground using GPS co-ordinates to find earthwork remains of demolished, neglected or forgotten features at Thorndon.

Regressive Mapping and Site Survey

The starting point for historic mapping was the 25 inch to the mile Ordnance Survey (OS) map of 1868. The features identified on these maps included the menagerie plantation, Hatch Farm, the pigeon mount, the old hall

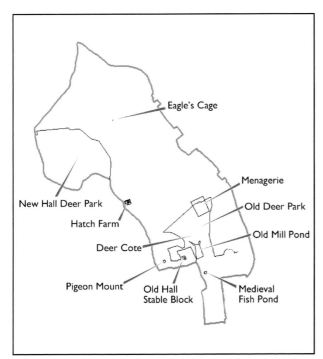

Figure 1 Features Associated with Animals at Thorndon Park. (Author's image.)

stables site and surviving relict buildings and earthworks. Other references on these maps included lost structures such as a deer cote and an eagle's cage, with further references, through place name evidence, to a rookery, paddocks and pastures. The maps also showed two deer parks associated with the old and new halls, in addition to place names such as, 'Old Thorndon Pasture' within or adjacent to the estate boundaries. Pastures indicate grazing by animals such as cattle and sheep, whereas paddocks would be associated with horses or deer.[7] Both the new and old halls had ponds, presumably for providing fish to the kitchens, water for grazing animals, and ornamentation to the landscaped grounds. The Home Farm was outside Thorndon (West Horndon) on the East Horndon Estate, with the farmland of these two manors amounting to 1,448 acres (most of which was rough pasture or parkland, partly leased to outlying farms).

Thorndon was completely remodelled from 1763 when the old hall was demolished and Lancelot Brown redesigned the park 1766-72, (although many of the landscape features now survive as archaeological remains). The Spyres map (1778) shows this re-arrangement of the landscape, including the menagerie *(Figure 11)*. This period also saw the demolition of the old hall, stables, outbuildings and St Nicholas Church.[8] The 1733 alignment faced north, but after 1772 the new hall faced south, with a new deer park to the west. Some features were retained from the Bourginion layout (see below), including the old deer park, menagerie, a serpentine lake feature and the mill pond *(Figure 10)*. Hatch Farm and Rookery Wood (the former location of the nursery) appeared on Spyres map of 1778,[9] with additional references to a northern Eagle's Cage (TQ58, TQ59) and a southern Deer cote (TQ68, TQ69) found on the OS 1:2500 maps (1868). The pigeon mount was also retained although the structure on this feature disap-

peared, and speculation suggests it may have fallen into disrepair, becoming another outbuilding, demolished with the old hall and its surrounding complex.[10]

The Bourginion plan (1733) for the formal gardens (only parts of which were actually constructed) included the 'esplanade', new Ingrave church, pleasure gardens adjacent to the old hall, the menagerie, nurseries, ponds, the enlargement of the old mill pond and the construction of a 'zigurat' between the northern arms, octagon, kitchen gardens and lawns. The stable block is to the east of the old hall, with gate houses to the east and west of the old hall *(Figure 1)*.[11] The menagerie was a feature of Robert James Petre's vision for Thorndon in the eighteenth century. It was approximately 180m square, with a central pond an island, animal sheds in the north east corner.

The pigeon mount did not appear on the Walker map of 1598, but was on the 1669 map by Duke Cosmo of Tuscany, and its interpretation suggests either a dovecote or a pergola.[12]

The Walker map (1598) included a pond situated east of the old hall, approximately 200m long by 90m wide and aligned north-south, which was most likely an integral part of a water management system which fed the moat. In addition, it served as a mill pond and fishpond; the northern arms were created while the main body had its capacity increased. The Walker map also showed the stable block associated with the old hall. During the present study large scatterings of Tudor brick, tiles and pottery were also found around Ruin Wood.[13]

Conclusions from Map Analysis:

Results from the map analysis provided an insight into how a major manorial estate connected with its animals for economic purposes, and into the social ideals by which livestock served as an ornamental feature to reflect family status. The Walker map (1598) demonstrates the Petre family's dominance over the surrounding landscape *(Figure 2)*; annotations such as 'Stable Mead' and 'The Oulde Parke' suggest the presence of high status animals such as horses and deer. The Bourginion map (1733) shows the planned changes proposed by Robert James Petre, retaining the deer park, the pigeon mount (possible dovecote) and the menagerie. The next detailed survey was carried out by Spyres (1778) after the estate had been re-arranged by Robert Edward Petre (1763) and Lancelot Brown (1766-72). The old deer park and menagerie were retained; the park was rotated through 180° and the new hall had a new deer park and pond installed.

The Spyres map also showed Hatch Farm inside the park boundaries. This specialist deer and cattle rearing farm also reflects the elite status of its surrounding landscape. Rookery Wood originates from the tree nursery, probably after Robert James's death in 1742.[14] The Claton map (1805) shows the menagerie, Hatch Farm, old pond and extensive parkland, but provides little additional detail.

The 1st edition OS (1868) identified a deer cote, north of the old pond, and Eagles Cage, west of the new hall. These suggest continuity of use and status.

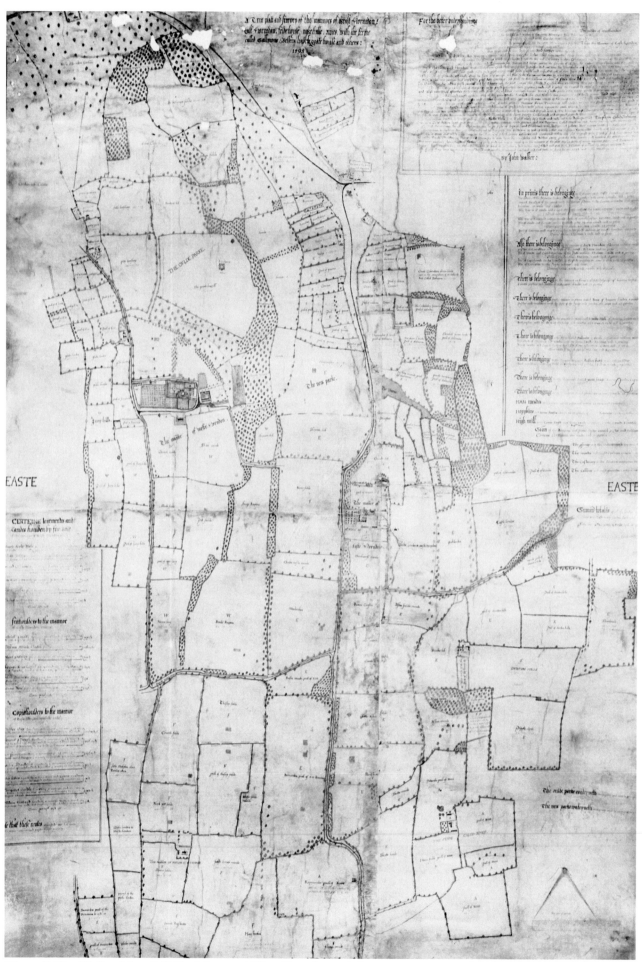

Figure 2 The Walker Map (1598) of East and West Horndon (ERO D/DP P5) (Reproduced by courtesy of Essex Record Office.)

84

Figure 3 Horsechestnut tree at the centre of Menagerie plateau, possibly 317 years old.

Earthworks Associated with Animal Structures and Management at Thorndon

The structural elements of Thorndon associated with animals in the landscape which remain as earthworks (*Figure 4*)[15] were examined during the surveying stages of this project. The archaeological survey carried out by Essex County Council (1994) made it possible to establish the position of the old hall stables, the menagerie and water management features.

Medieval Fish Pond

The earthworks of possible medieval fish ponds in Mill Wood pre-date the Petre family's ownership of Thorndon. They have been recorded by Essex County Council and were investigated again during this survey. This feature was very overgrown with vegetation but showed up clearly through mapping, using the OS contour and spot height data. The first survey identified its ground position and map analysis using GIS showed a depression inside the 30m contour with a bank, also at 30m, separating the remains of a possible pond. The first survey identified features which correlated with Clutton and Mackay (1970) and the ECC archaeological report (1994); these features were investigated further during the second survey. This feature comprised a shallow

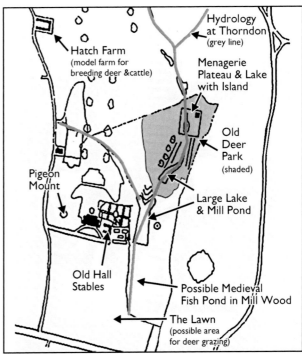

Figure 4 Garden Elements at the southern end of Thorndon 1733-42, in Clutton and Mackay (1970b).

depression, approximately 1m deep, with a possible second pond to the south, although the natural topography drops away south. The spot heights indicate a 30m bank running east to west across this feature which appeared man made (because it was straight), and a possible gully connecting the stream on the western side, which could indicate a water management system (as shown in *Figure 5*).

Menagerie

Rectangular earthworks to the north were recorded as an enclosure for animals. These comprise a slight ditch and bank forming a right-angle at the north-west corner, a centrally located, landscaped pond, and traces of a dam across the stream to the south.[16] Field study also showed a deep cut earthwork, possible remains of a sluice gate. The menagerie terracing (*Figure 6*) steps up three times from the stream, before levelling out to form the plateau where the animal enclosures were reported to be.[17]

The large horse chestnut tree, central to the menagerie

Figure 5 Mill Wood Earthworks.

Figure 6 Terraced Earthworks leading to the Menagerie Plateau.

Figure 7 Plateau in front of Ruin Wood, position of gate house and entrance driveway.

plateau, had a girth measurement of 430cm. The Forestry Commission's tree dating calculation places this tree at 317 years old, with a planting date of 1692. Taking this age and date as accurate, this would suggest that it was selected as a shade tree, around 35-40 years old and close to animal structures in Lord Petre's Menagerie *(Figure 3)*.

Pond Associated with Mill and Menagerie

Relict evidence of water management, and natural hydro-logical data, provided clues for finding structures and areas associated with animals.[18] The earliest suggested evidence of water management was found at Mill Wood, where the depressions and gullies appear to connect with the stream *(Figure 3)* running from the north and west, heading south *(Figure 2)*. The menagerie also followed this line of natural hydrology with its pond acting as part of the water management system to the north of a large serpentine lake and mill pond. A bridge across the stream, containing a three course arch and ten plus stretcher courses, could have been for carriage traffic visiting the menagerie. Another feature noted was an earthwork within Mill Wood, thought to be a medieval fishpond or possibly a quarry site, which shows up as rectangular depressions and banks – but no documentary evidence for this has been found.[19] Traces of a watering system for Robert James Petre's nursery remain as earthworks in the area now known as the Rookery.

Figure 9 Feature resembling the Island and Lake of the Thorndon Menagerie.

Figure 8 Earthwork terrace and plateau, most probably associated with the old stable block at Thorndon. Note the tree cover which created difficulties. GPS readings were still possible under light tree cover, although the accuracy was reduced.

Bridge

The bridge *(Figure 10)* was re-examined. Its three course arch and ten plus stretcher courses strongly suggest that the driveway and entrance to the menagerie were on the northern side of the plateau, but no dating evidence was available at the time of surveying. The pond, island and animal enclosure would all have been visible from the bridge position, with the drive heading up the hill toward the possible site entrance.

Stables

Stables were situated south-east of the old hall, visible to travellers heading north from the Thames *(Figure 7)*; the pigeon mount on a terraced plateau and the lawn extended south beyond them. Walking this area revealed no obvious remains of the stables except a terrace in front of Ruin Wood, so during the second survey GPS co-ordinates were used to locate their position on the ground. Reviewing the map evidence between surveys located the stables *(Figure 8)* east of Ruin Wood on a slightly lower plateau to the old hall, as illustrated on Walker's map (1598). The first survey produced useful

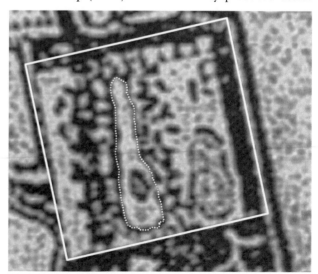

Figure 10 Bourginion (1733) menagerie layout. (ERO D/DP 23/1, detail) (Reproduced by courtesy of Essex Record Office.)

data on Thorndon's layout, but to ensure accuracy this was cross-referenced with a second site visit to pinpoint features on the ground. To achieve this, mapping from Clutton and Mackay's (1970) study of Old Thorndon Hall was scanned, then overlaid onto OS maps to establish the correct scale and orientation, before making comparisons with historic estate maps. This allowed GPS co-ordinates to be generated in GIS, which in turn provided a system for cross-referencing actual ground positions with points generated during the survey exercise. These processes led to the interpretation that the plateau to the east of ruin wood was the most likely location for the old stable block *(Figure 8)*.

Pigeon Mount

The pigeon mount, positioned approximately 200m west from the old hall survives as a sizeable earthwork about 30m in diameter and 4m high. Its purpose is unknown, although suggestions include a dovecote or pergola as possibilities.[20] The pigeon mount was excavated in the 1990s. This revealed an octagonal building constructed of brick. Window glass and lead indicated diamond pattern windows in the walls or dormers in the roof. The pegged and hipped roof tiles conform to the construction techniques required for an octagonal building.[21] The recovery of slip glazed tile suggested an ornate floor was once in place. The absence of plaster, render or pointing of the brickwork does not fit with an ornately decorated building such as a summer house, therefore the tiles could have been a practical way of keeping the floor clean. The lack of interior plaster could indicate that the building was lined with some other material, such as fired clay or pre-formed nesting boxes, which have been noted in dovecotes on other sites. Large pieces of shaped, baked clay or daub remain unexplained. This fired ceramic material could be from pre-formed nesting units. The octagonal dovecote was a popular architectural variation in the seventeenth and eighteenth century, as were free-standing, ornately decorated dovecotes, created as landscape features. Furthermore, pigeons were thought to prefer light, airy conditions, therefore it was not uncommon for dovecotes to contain windows.[22]

During the first survey, fragments of Tudor brick and glazed floor tiles were found in the eroding soil of the slopes of the pigeon mount.

The Lawn and Southern Hedge

The lawn was ploughed when surveying took place, but the field boundaries had not changed since Clutton and Mackay's map was drawn (1970, *Figure 4*). Although it looked different on Bourginion's plan (1733), its position correlated with this map. The southern hedge *(Figure 7)* appears to be much later, as it would have obscured views of St Nicholas Church (now demolished), the lawn and the Thames, but the field boundary itself was on Walker's map (1598).

Menagerie Lake and Island

The process of cross-checking between map and survey was used to search for the island and lake associated with the menagerie (northeast of the old deer park). As outlined above, the first survey located the plateau and terracing of the menagerie, but did not locate the island and lake. Difficulties inherent with GPS and geo-referencing of documentary evidence caused errors, which had to be taken into account during ground-proofing exercises. In addition, GPS – however advanced it may be – does not work well under tree canopies because the satellite signals become interrupted when the line of sight is poor and inaccuracies occur. For these reasons, finding the stable block in open ground *(Figure 8)* was easier then finding the island and lake of the menagerie *(Figure 9)*, but the combination of technology and field work has manage to identify a feature likely to be the island and lake.

Archival Research

Some original research was carried out on references to animals in the Thorndon archives, and this was combined with material taken from the 1972 publication on Old Thorndon by J. Ward based on documentary evidence.

Sixteenth Century

'The Stables, Barns and Coach-houses at Thorndon stood at a little distance from the dwelling house, and surrounded three sides of a yard … Work began there in September, 1587, when brickbats were gathered from the rubbish to serve for the foundations of the new barns and stables the following year, and work was in progress throughout 1589-90. In autumn of 1589, the roof of the east end of the great stable, and little stable and the two coach-houses, and the two long stables, and saddle-house, were framed and raised. Brick was being laid at the new stables, barns and coach-houses, and the coach-house and stables were being tiled in the early winter. The work was progressing well when, on the Twelfth Night, 1590, a great wind so badly cracked and shook the brick walls of the new stables that they had to be completely taken down. The damaged tiles on the dwelling-house and outhouses were replaced in mid-February; work on the stables began again in the spring.'[23]

The estate in the sixteenth century was alive with the near constant movement of horses '…from dawn to dusk, and longer, there were horses to be accommodated.'[24] Lonely and Lion lodges were the homes to the warrener and gamekeeper respectively,[25] later becoming private houses.

The bailiff of husbandry was responsible for Home Farm, under the supervision of John Bentley from 1573. The records show that cattle were bought and sold for beef, although a dairy herd was kept to supply the household with milk, veal and beef, with hides being sold to local tanners. In addition, a moderate size flock of sheep was kept for wool, meat and sale.[26] A falconer was employed by Sir William Petre from 1550, and there are references to a 'mews'.[27]

'Sparrow hawks bred in the wooded parts of the old park, and a watch was kept on them for an opportunity to seize young birds to replenish the mews'.[28]

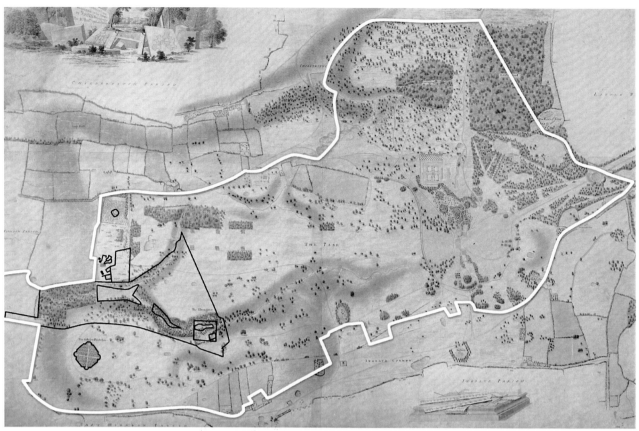

Figure 11 *Spyres map of Thorndon (1778) with Stables (1598) and modification to the designed landscape (1733) overlaid: (ERO D/DP P30) (Reproduced by courtesy of Essex Record Office.)*

Seventeenth Century:

References in the archival records and accounts of Thorndon reveal an estate focused on livestock, with cattle, sheep and deer providing food and income. Cattle sales in 1655-56 exceeded £1,000 and new stock cost around £500.[29]

Quarter Session records provide insights into the poaching of deer in the seventeenth century. Archive records of 1655-63 suggest that Thorndon's deer park was still busy after nightfall, with local people trespassing with regularity. On 20 March 1655 (Q/SR 366/18) a warrant was issued for the arrest of Richard Larder for killing deer in Thorndon. Larder was arrested but escaped custody.[30] On 29 December 1655 (Q/SR 367/45) Henry Barnard, Thomas Barnard and Robert Luken were charged with unlawful hunting and killing of deer at Thorndon.[31] More detailed accounts from 1661-63 show regular poaching by a gang of three to five men with dogs, with John Radley's name appearing in March 1661 and again in December 1663. In 1661 (Q/SR 388/14, 17 and Q/SR 388/22) Radley was accused of illegal entry to Thorndon to hunt and kill deer. These sources also describe his dogs as being well known to the local community, but kept at residences not occupied by Radley.[32]

Eighteenth Century

The stables were very busy. Servants started at 5am and the cleaning, feeding, watering and exercising of the horses had to be completed before breakfast. Accounts record servants deliberately pulling off horseshoes to provide an excuse to visit the smith – and the ale house while they waited.[33] Horse feed was given out by a bailiff or steward every Monday morning to coachmen and grooms, who were allowed two bushels of oats for each horse under their care.[34]

The Thorndon accounts from 1766 to 1778 indicate that the menagerie was staffed by Dominic Wood and his wife Francis during this period, with their combined earnings totalling £12 10s per half year. Dominic was possibly the best paid member of Lord Petre's staff who worked with animals, earning £20 per annum over this twelve year period. Thomas Vincent the farmer (£7 10s 0d), William Gibbs the groom (£7 0s 0d), John Robson the second farmer (£5 5s 0d), James Digby the under groom (£4 10s 0d) and Elizabeth Kiteheen the dairy maid (£4 0s 0d) were all earning lower half-yearly incomes.[35] The menagerie was still being maintained in 1788, but work was carried out by day workers.[36] Accounts recorded repairs to the earthworks and structures, but no reference to an animal keeper. The six-monthly contracts shown in D/DP/A167 do not show up in the D/DP/A59 estate accounts, which only listed day workers and no regular staff.

It is also recorded that Robert James received some 'Olive Birds' despatched to Thorndon's menagerie. Collinson and Bartram were linked to these purchases from America.[37] The menagerie plantation '... at Thorndon included ornamental ducks and pheasants, deer, sheep, red fowl from New England ... terrapins, bustards ... squirrels. These were either let loose in the park and adjoining woods or else kept in the menagerie ...'[38]

Nineteenth Century

A letter dated 1860 thanks Lord Petre for sending red deer to the Clifford family in New Zealand. It is signed by John Morrison, whose family settled in the colony (1860).[39]

Discussion of Archival Material:

Archival and literary documentation assisted the visual analysis of map evidence by providing details of individual features, but it also helped to understand the social, political and economic situation of contemporary lives. Thorndon's lord was very rich and provided employment to servants and supported the parish economy – in fact the family's influence extended far beyond Thorndon's manorial jurisdiction. Animals were one way to demonstrate this power and Thorndon certainly exhibited elite family status through the keeping of deer, the employment of a falconer and a warrener, and the presence of fish ponds, which were all privileges of the elite class. Collections of exotic animals, kept in menageries, reflected fashionable trends as well as demonstrating the ability to reach out across the known world to bring back unknown animals or plants for domestication or display purposes. Robert James Petre was famous for his connection with America and his passion for exotic plant and animal species.[40]

Conclusion

This research has confirmed the importance of utilising the full range of documentary, archaeological, cartographic and GIS technology to achieve a complete picture of the landscape. Survey work was based on map and documentary evidence and these processes were enhanced by GIS technology, which allowed re-scaling and correlation of estate maps to provide overlays on modern OS maps. GIS provided mapping for the first survey, allowed the processing of results between surveys, and provided data for pinning down the locations of structures, not accurately known by generating GPS co-ordinates to be cross-referenced during the second survey. This 'tracking' process confirmed the positions of the stable block and the menagerie island by re-examining earthworks that were overlooked or missed during the first survey. The use of handheld GPS, in conjunction with co-ordinates generated by GIS mapping, narrowed the search area down to approximately a 10m radius.

Once the search area had been narrowed down, features that appeared as meaningless earthworks started to correlate with the mapping and documentary evidence, and careful examination revealed their true characteristics. The position of old hall stables appeared obvious when all the evidence was compiled and cross-referenced. The menagerie was more difficult, because its complexity and scale were hidden within two hundred years' growth of woodland vegetation, but reducing the search area was beneficial to earthwork interpretation. The terracing and menagerie plateau were identified during the first survey, but the lake remained obscured by undergrowth until the second survey narrowed the search area down. These earthworks were viewed from the west on the first survey and from the east on the second survey. These anomalies stood out better because, seen from the east, higher ground looked down on the earthworks, and because additional data had been compiled before walking the area.

Management of animals at Thorndon extends back at least four hundred years. Thorndon's ownership remained in one family from 1573 until the mid-twentieth century, becoming symbolic of an elite manorial landscape. This parkland landscape changed, most noticeably in the eighteenth century, but animals remained a key theme in the management strategy and economic sustainability of Thorndon and its surrounding parishes. Thorndon's location also allowed access to London's markets and ports, enabling the Petre family's influence to extend beyond England to the known world. This was demonstrated in the eighteenth century by Robert James Petre's introduction of plants and animals from America and the establishment of a plant nursery as well as the menagerie incorporated into Thorndon's landscape in 1733.

The presence of a falconer, fish ponds and the keeping of deer were rights associated with privilege. These rights were evident from the 1570s when the family purchased the Thorndon and Ingatestone estates. References to Lonely Lodge, the warrener residence, the pigeon mount, a possible dovecote and the stables also evoke manorial benefits and family status. No evidence of warrens were found and the pigeon mount's use is speculative, but their reference should still be considered within the theme of investigating structures associated with animals. Equally, the presence of domestic animals such as sheep and cattle cannot be overlooked, especially as they provided food, income, employment along with resources to Thorndon's estate and surrounding parishes. Animals clearly had great significance within Thorndon's landscape for many reasons associated with estate management, but also – as the Quarter Session records show – there were unwanted animals present, particularly those used for poaching deer.

Thorndon's estate was a living landscape and supports the evidence put forward by Festing, Groves and others, that manorial estates had strong links with animals, to demonstrate family status, fashion, and contemporary design theory. The historical evidence has faded with time, but remains in the documentation, structural relics, earthworks and vegetation of this protected landscape. Thorndon's landscape today is still open parkland and its historical themes are demonstrated through interpretation panels for the visiting public. Essex County Council currently owns a large proportion of Thorndon Park and protects this listed, relict landscape and its connections to grazing and free-roaming deer. The old and new deer parks remain and animals are still an attraction at Thorndon with goat paddocks in the northern (new) deer park. The field boundaries, south of Childerditch Common and west of Thorndon Park, have not changed since the Walker map was drawn in 1598. The menagerie and old deer park are now SSSIs and animal grazing areas maintaining the connections with animals, which had great significance to Thorndon's landscape history. The combination of poor soils and emphasis on grazing and parkland contributed to the survival of Thorndon's landscape features, helping them escape the plough – so its history lives on for the public to appreciate today.

Bibliography

Clutton, Sir, G., 1970a 'The Death and Fame of Robert James, 8th Lord Petre' in *Essex Journal*, 5, 57-61

Clutton, Sir. G. & Mackay C., 1970b 'Old Thorndon Hall, Essex: An History and Reconstruction on its Park and Garden' in *Historic Gardens*, 12, 27-39

Edwards, A.C., 1975 *John Petre*, London

Essex County Council, 1994 *Country Parks Archaeological Survey Thorndon Park*, ECC Planning Department Archaeological Advisory Group, 1-32

Essex County Council, 1995 *The Pigeon Mount, Thorndon Park, Brentwood*, ECC Field Archaeology Unit

Essex Field Club, 2004 *Essex Park*, Stratford

Festing, S., 1988 'Menageries and the landscape gardens', in *Garden History*, 8, 104-117.

Groves, L., 2002 Animals: Living Garden Features Not Incidental Occupants, unpublished MA Dissertation, Birkbeck University

Harvey, N., 1984 *A History of Farm Buildings in England and Wales*, David and Charles

Hicks, D., & Beaudry M.C., 2006 *The Cambridge Companion to Historical Archaeology*, Cambridge

Muir, R., 2000 *The New Reading of the Landscape: Fieldwork in Landscape History*, Exeter

Symes, M., 2006 *A Glossary of Garden History*, Shire Books

Ward, J. C., 1972 *The History of Old Thorndon Hall*, Essex County Council

Primary Sources are referenced in the text

References

1   Groves 2002
2   Symes 2006
3   Festing 1988, 104-117
4   Edwards 1975
5   Essex Field Club 2004
6   Hicks & Beaudry 2006
7   Muir 2000
8   Essex County Council, 1994, 1-32
9   Ibid, 1994.
10 Ibid, 1994.
11 Essex County Council 1994, 1-32.
12 Essex County Council 1995
13 Essex County Council 1994, 1-32
14 Clutton & Mackay 1970b, 27-39
15 Clutton & Mackay 1970b, 27-39
16 ESMR, in Essex County Council 1994, 1-32
17 Essex County Council 1994, 1-32
18 Harvey 1984
19 ESMR, in Essex County Council 1994, 1-32
20 ESMR, in Essex County Council 1994, 1-32
21 Ibid, 1994.
22 Ibid, 1994.
23 Ward 1972
24 Edwards 1975
25 Edwards, 1975
26 Edwards 1975
27 Ibid, 33
28 Ibid, 49
29 ERO. D/DP/A53, (1655-56)
30 ERO. Q/SR 366/18, (1655)
31 ERO. Q/SR 367/45, (1655)
32 ERO. Q/SR 388/22, (1661)
33 ERO..D/DP/F375, (1740), 4
34 ERO..D/DP/F375, (1740), 7
35 ERO. D/DP/A167, (1766-78)
36 ERO. D/DP/A59, (1788)
37 Clutton 1970a, 57-61
38 Clutton & Mackay 1970b, 27-39
39 ERO. D/DP E174, (1860)
40 Clutton & Mackay, 1970a 57-61